It's a Small World After All

"You are from America?"

I nodded.

"Then perhaps you know a friend of mine. He lives in Chicago."

"What's his name?" I asked.

My husband stared at me in astonishment. "Are you crazy?" he whispered. "Do you know the odds of—"

"His name is Joe," said the clerk.

"I only know one Joe in Chicago," I said.

"It's probably him." He smiled.

•   •   •

Books by Erma Bombeck

At Wit's End
"Just Wait Till You Have Children of Your Own!"
I Lost Everything in the Post-Natal Depression
The Grass Is Always Greener Over the Septic Tank
If Life Is a Bowl of Cherries, What Am I Doing in the Pits?
Aunt Erma's Cope Book
Motherhood: The Second Oldest Profession
Family: The Ties That Bind . . . and Gag!
I Want to Grow Hair, I Want to Grow Up, I Want to Go to Boise *
When You Look Like Your Passport Photo, It's Time To Go Home *

*Published by
HarperPaperbacks

Erma Bombeck

When You Look Like Your Passport Photo, It's Time To Go Home

HarperPaperbacks
A Division of HarperCollinsPublishers

HarperPaperbacks   *A Division of* HarperCollins*Publishers*
10 East 53rd Street, New York, N.Y. 10022

A hardcover edition of this book was published in1991 by HarperCollins*Publishers.*

Cover design by Mike Stromberg
Cover photo by Steve Van Warner

First HarperPaperbacks printing: November 1992

Printed in the United States of America

HarperPaperbacks and colophon are trademarks of HarperCollins*Publishers*

❖ 10 9 8 7 6 5 4 3 2 1

Contents

Contents

Contents

Papua
New Guinea

The gunshots started about two in the morning. They were followed closely by the sounds of broken bottles being thrown at the hotel and screams from the room next door. Lying next to me in bed was a lunatic who brought me to this place to shed the stress of kids, phones, and meal-planning anxiety.

This was the third week of our vacation in Papua New Guinea, and my husband and I were in the middle of a tribal war in a small village called Kundiawa.

In the lull, we both stared at the ceiling of the dark room, not daring to move. "Call me crazy," I said, "but I don't think these people have a handle on tourism."

My husband breathed deeply. "I've told you

before, the fighting has nothing to do with us. It's between two tribes."

"You do have a way of turning gray skies into blue," I said flatly.

A dog barked. In the hallway outside our door, there were hurried footsteps and shouting that faded quickly.

"Did you know there is no water in this hotel?" I asked.

"How many times do I have to tell you, this is a third-world country. You can't expect to have a mint on your pillow every night. You have to appreciate the primitive charm of this place."

"Do you think it's safe to crawl across the floor to the bathroom?"

"No," he said and turned over to sleep.

I couldn't close my eyes. What was I doing here? I was a woman who washed her tennis shoes every week sleeping on a pillow without a case. A woman who hyperventilated when she found a roach in her grocery bag sharing a park restroom with a snake coiled just above the commode. A woman who brought one nice dress with her to wear to church on Sundays only to discover the natives went to Mass topless. God, I hated being overdressed!

Vacations always sound so great on paper. They are supposed to save your marriage, save your sanity, bring about understanding in the world, clear up your skin—all those things. The truth is if you do them right, they're hard work. They're like an Outward Bound experience with diarrhea. We pay a lot of money to sleep in airports, lug around suitcases twice our body weight, eat food we can't identify, and put our lives in the hands of people we have never met before.

In more than twenty years of traveling, I had to admit, Papua New Guinea was the most unusual culture I had ever witnessed. I know that because my husband told me so. He is like one of those talking cassettes where you hit a button and it spews out details of what you are seeing. Just push on his navel and you'll hear, "On May 27, 1930, Papua New Guinea became the last inhabited region on the planet to be explored by Europeans." He will also tell you it is crucial to see all of this before civilization dumps its technology on it in the name of progress.

When he delivered that soliloquy, we were standing on a dirt street in the center of Goroko where people had their pigs on leashes. Somehow I didn't feel the threat was imminent.

Their driving laws weren't exactly out of an AAA manual. If you are involved in an accident in Papua New Guinea, don't stop. Keep going until you reach the nearest police station. There is a payback law by which the wronged person randomly selects the next person matching your skin color and kills him. If you hit a pig, don't even think of pausing to make restitution, but go to the police. "And don't forget," my husband warned, "if you see people walking with axes, knives, or bows and arrows, do not stop. Keep moving."

I remember staring at him and saying, "You have just ruined my surprise."

Another gunshot cracked into the night. I shook my husband awake. "Are you wearing your Mickey Mouse underwear today?"

"Yes," he said sleepily.

"Then tomorrow must be Wednesday . . . Joe Palooka day."

"Try to get some sleep," he said. He resumed snoring.

The underwear. It had all seemed so long ago since we arrived here. We were scheduled to stop off in Papeete in Tahiti for a couple of days to get over jet lag before pushing on to Port Moresby. I remember it was eleven o'clock at night when the luggage carousel ground to a sickening halt and we realized we were the last two people there. I had my luggage, but my husband had the look of a man who had just had his life-support system removed.

"My luggage! It's not here," he gasped. "It's probably still on the plane here in Tahiti. I'm going to check on it before the plane takes off."

I grabbed his arm. "Grow up! It's not still on the plane. It's probably back in Phoenix."

"Everything I own is in those suitcases. My binoculars, my film, all my clothes and toiletries."

"Did I ever tell you about that grandmother from Fort Lauderdale?"

"Yes," he said miserably, looking for an agent.

"She was going to her grandson's wedding in Pittsburgh and her luggage went to Canada?"

"You told me," he said.

"The airline told her if she didn't receive her luggage in twenty-four hours, she would receive $35 for new underwear, but that was the least of her problems because all she had to wear to the wedding were the slack suit and sneakers she had traveled in. Are you sure I didn't tell you this?"

"Do you see a representative of the airline anywhere?"

"Anyway," I continued, "the family tried to come to the rescue, but the mother of the bride was too short and too thin, so she finally ended up in something that fit—a blue maternity dress. They washed out the old spots and dried it with a hair dryer and she marched down the aisle between her two grandsons wearing a maternity dress and a pair of gold bedroom slippers."

"Make your point," he said, irritably shuffling through the claim forms.

"The point is we are en route to Papua New Guinea for a trip down the Sepik River and you are dressed like an investment broker."

"The luggage will show up," he said.

My last words on the subject were "In your dreams."

He had ignored the first commandment of
adventurers everywhere, "Thou shalt not travel
with anything thou cannot carry at a dead run for
half a mile and store under thy seat." He was
learning firsthand what a man in St. Louis found
out when he told the ticket agent he was going to
Dallas and asked, "Can you check my luggage
through to Honolulu and Passaic, New Jersey,
first?" When the agent said he couldn't do that,
the passenger replied, "Funny, you routed it there
last week."

Two days passed in Tahiti . . . two days of
lounging around the pool in a business suit. I told
him, "Stick a lamp cord in your ear and everyone
will think you're a Secret Service agent." On the
fourth day out, I convinced him his luggage had
gone to that big Bermuda Triangle in the sky. He
simply had to go shopping.

Port Moresby looked like the best shot to pull
together a wardrobe, considering it is the capital
city of Papua New Guinea and the main gateway
to the South Pacific. It would probably offer the
best shopping before we went into the highlands
of the Wahgi Valley, the small towns of Lae and
Madang, or the primitive villages dotting the
Sepik River. We expected the selection of clothes
to be limited. That was a given. But we didn't
anticipate the real problem of shopping in Port
Moresby.

Papua New Guinea has an indigenous population. Its people are the products of dozens of ethnic groups, mostly Melanesians. There are bearded highlanders, hook-nose lowlanders, men who wear body armor, wig men, mud men, warriors, fishermen, farmers, and mountaineers. With the exception of the people of the North Solomons, they all have one thing in common. They are short. Real short. They don't walk under coffee tables, but most of them are no more than four feet tall.

When my husband, who is six feet tall and wears a size twelve shoe, walked into the menswear department in Port Moresby, the salesman didn't know whether to launch him or erect him in the center of town and direct traffic around him. In metric, he was awesome. There are a few Australians in the city, but mostly you're looking at little people who go around talking earnestly to belt buckles.

I must also add that Papuan New Guineans are the world's friendliest people. Upon meeting you they will grasp your hand excitedly, say good morning, and begin a conversation. (In the bush the greetings are a little more graphic. Women push in your chest with both of their hands. When I asked how the men greeted one another, our guide said, "You don't want to know.")

As my husband flipped through the racks of little shirts and troll shorts, he said, "This has got to be the boys' department."

"No, no, it's for men," said our salesperson, a

young kid who never stopped smiling. During a lull, he turned to me and said, "Did you know that Number One Jesus Man was just here?"

"And who would that be?" I asked.

"The Pope. Do you know him? He came to Port Moresby and kissed the ground."

I told him I had not had the pleasure.

Then he observed, "You are from America?" I nodded. "Then perhaps you know a friend of mine. He lives in Chicago."

"What's his name?" I asked.

My husband stared at me astonished. "Are you crazy?" he whispered. "Do you know the odds of—"

"His name is Joe," said the clerk.

"I only know one Joe in Chicago," I said.

"It's probably him." He smiled.

I waited on a small chair while my husband paraded in and out of the dressing room in one little outfit after another looking for approval. After several pairs of trousers that would have seen him through a Texas flood, I said, "I'm telling you this as a friend. Stick to the shorts."

Reinforced by a gym bag filled with underwear emblazoned in old comic strip characters, a couple pairs of shorts, and a few T-shirts, we embarked on our first adventure through a country where women are considered currency and isolated ceremonial cannibalism was practiced as recently as the 1950s.

If nothing else, the limited wardrobe took away major decisions. We measured time by my husband's underwear. Every Monday he wore the Blondie and Dagwood print while Tuesday's Mickey Mouse print was drying and Wednesday's Joe Palooka was being washed.

The drive through the highlands was incredibly lush and beautiful. At one point our driver pointed out a remote spot where a plane had gone down several years ago. "The natives saw it fall to the ground," he said, "and when they got there, two were still alive."

"They took them to the hospital?" I asked.

"They ate them," he said.

It gave new meaning to the catch-of-the-day.

We stopped at a few burial caves where villagers inter their family by propping the skeletons up on a ledge or leaning them against the wall. It reminded me of a spa in California where I spent a week once, but that's another chapter.

In retrospect, if you have to lose your luggage, traveling down the Sepik River is the best place to lose it. It's a fairly laid-back country that gives a California lifestyle the pomp of a coronation. There were ten of us—mostly Australians—who boarded the *Melanesian Explorer* for our trip down the Sepik.

The ship was comfortable and clean, but it had an *African Queen* quality to it. I say this because we boarded right after dinner one night in Madang and when we awakened, I strolled out on deck with a cup of coffee only to realize we hadn't left the dock yet. Humphrey Bogart was still fixing the motor.

The cabins were air conditioned and were listed in the brochure as having showers, but all I saw was a toilet. When I mentioned this to my husband, he said, "Look up." I hadn't done that since the snake incident. But sure enough, a small nozzle came out of the ceiling, making it possible to sit on the commode and shower at the same time if you were on a tight schedule.

Ironically, I had no trouble filling my time on the *Explorer*. I read and slept, and one night a mosquito asked me to dance after dinner.

A word about mosquitoes. There are two kinds of people in this world: those who do not attract mosquitoes and those who do. I not only belong to the second group, but I have documented proof that mosquitoes actually subscribe to a newsletter telling the whereabouts of feasts like me. They then book passage on commercial planes (first class) and get to wherever I am.

People think mosquitoes are all alike. They are not. Alaskan mosquitoes are equipped with rotary blades like a helicopter. They will hover two inches from your face and hum like a barbershop harmony convention in progress.

In the South Pacific, because of their size,

mosquitoes are required to file flight plans. They make virtually little sound. The only hint you have that your entire body is under attack is that your tan goes pale. It's like giving blood at the Red Cross without the cookie.

In between navigating the river, we would stop off at small villages and visit large two-story structures called Haus Tambarans. These are where the talents of the Sepik flourish: wood carvings, jewelry, primitive masks, and story boards crafted by local artisans. The natives have a unique way of bargaining you never see in any other part of the world. I picked up a rough-hewn carving of a mother and child and asked, "How much?" The man smiled and recited in perfect English, "First price, $300. Second price, $80." He waited anxiously for my decision.

Sometimes at night when you entered a village by torchlight because there was no electricity or you watched the men of the village digging out a new canoe while their children splashed naked in the river, you had a fierce urge to protect all of it from hemorrhoid commercials and Golden Arches. After a while, you even stopped fighting the inconveniences and gave in to them. I got used to being the only non–nursing mother in an airport. If the plane was full, a "frequent flyer" wearing nothing but "arse grass" around his waist (which is exactly what it sounds like) would smile a red betel-nut smile, pull a sack of onions into the aisle, and sit down beside you. (Hey, they'd put their mothers in the overhead racks if that's all the room that was left.)

At an open market one day, a Papuan New Guinean asked if I had a husband. I assured him I did. I couldn't believe he asked me to point him out. You could hardly miss him. He was the one with the whitest legs in North America and the only one in the country taller than a car.

"Are you his only wife?" he asked.

"Yes," I said. "We're Catholic."

He said he was too, and he had three wives. I wondered what the Number One Jesus Man would have thought about that.

As light reluctantly entered the room in Kundiawa, I realized with relief that things had quieted down a bit. It had been a while since I heard glass shatter or guns explode. I felt rotten. My head ached, my body alternated with chills and fever. Occasionally, my bones felt like someone was snapping them in half. Crawling along the floor until I reached the bathroom, I switched on the light. It was not a pretty sight. My eyes were bloodred and my vision wasn't great. My skin had a yellow pallor. I dropped to the floor and crawled back into bed where I shook my husband awake.

"I don't want to panic you, but I wanted to say goodbye and tell you your second wife will rot in hell before I tell her where my dinner ring is hidden. I harbor no bad feelings for being dragged to this godforsaken place where they have never heard of Liz Claiborne."

"It's stress." He yawned. "Try to get some sleep."

"Not until you tell me a story," I said stubbornly.

He took a deep breath. "All right, which one do you want to hear?"

"Tell me the one again about what we are doing here."

"Very well." He smiled. "But you've got to promise me that you'll go to sleep . . . no more stalling . . . no more drinks of water. . . ."

"There is no water," I reminded him.

"Right. Well, once upon a time, many many years ago, there was a young princess who lived in the suburban kingdom of Centerville, Ohio, with her handsome prince and their three children. It seemed like a storybook existence except every summer when all her friends went on journeys to magic places, she took care of their houses, brought in their mail, and fed their dogs. As if that wasn't bad enough, every summer the Semple family visited their cottage. . . ."

I quivered. "I always get a chill at this part."

"I know," he said softly. "As time went by the princess put her royal foot down and said, 'There has to be something more to summers than this! I'm going to travel all over the world and feast at the banquet table of life. . . .'"

I slept.

Centerville, Ohio

As the front door of Helen and Hal's house slammed shut, I deposited her house key in my slacks pocket like a matron at a maximum security prison. I didn't relish telling Helen and her family when they returned from Hawaii that their bird had died. Or that her Boston fern went into cardiac arrest the day after she left.

As I made my way across the yard connecting our houses, I wondered if Helen's mother would mention to her that when she dropped by to stock the refrigerator for their return, I thought she was an intruder and called the police. Silly me. Her mother had probably forgotten the incident by this time.

I tossed Helen's mail and her newspaper in a

cardboard box in the hallway by the front door and made a mental note that tomorrow I would have to eat the three bananas she had left on her drainboard. They were starting to attract fruit flies.

How many summers had I housesat for Helen? How many times had I waved goodbye as they honked their horn before they pulled out of the driveway headed for paradise? How many picturesque postcards had found their way to our mailbox? Our family never went on vacations. It was always something. No sooner would we get the Christmas bills under control than the transmission fell out of the car, the clothes dryer caught fire, or the orthodontist wanted $2,000 to straighten the teeth of a kid who never smiled anyway. This year it was, "Daddy! Daddy! Our grass is wet and squishy under my bedroom window and it smells!"

I didn't understand it. Helen and Hal didn't make any more money than we did, yet every year they pored over brochures, planned, saved, and traveled. The four of them returned invigorated and ready to face another fifty weeks of mortgage payments and car repairs.

We had had one vacation since our marriage. Because my husband was a social studies teacher, the senior class offered to pay our way for their class trip to Washington and New York if we would serve as chaperones. Someone should have warned us that the only place you can tour comfortably with thirty-five sexually active seniors is Arlington Cemetery. (And then only if you connect them to a single rope and have them walk in single file.)

A horn honked in the driveway, interrupting my moment of self-pity. It was the Semples, Howard, Fay, and their three kids . . . right on schedule.

The five of them stopped by every summer from Rochester, New York, on their way to visit Howard's brother in California. It was all too predictable. Fay would hop out of the car and say, "Let's get unpacked. We have so much to catch up on." We'd catch up after fifteen minutes and spend the rest of the time talking about gas mileage, lawn diseases, and people who died whom they said we remembered but we never knew. Actually, we didn't know Fay and Howard real well.

When they lived in Centerville, their daughter Sissy took piano lessons from the same teacher as my daughter. We met every year at the piano recital. For three years in a row, Sissy played "There's a Fairy in the Bottom of My Teacup." No one had the heart to tell the Semples the kid had reached the level of her incompetence. At one of these recitals, my husband inadvertently spilled punch down Fay's back. A conversation ensued. She told him that they were moving to Rochester because Howard had a job offer. My husband, Bill Inter-Continental, said, "Don't be a stranger. If you ever get back to Centerville, pop on by."

Fay carried her klutzy little makeup kit (which was never more than three feet away from her body) inside while I kicked one large suitcase on wheels and balanced a weekender and a duffel bag under each arm.

"Does Bill still spill drinks down women's backs?" She giggled.

"He does it for a living now." I smiled.

The Semple family was not without talents. Howard had been training for the gargling Olympics all of his life. Every day, he began just before the sun came up, continuing through breakfast and again in the evening when everyone was in bed trying to sleep.

Fay had a gift for becoming "domestically dead" the moment she walked out of her own home. She did not know how to start a washer or plug in an iron, and had no curiosity as to how to turn on a stove. She just looked helpless all the time and whimpered, "If I knew where things went, I'd put them away" and then walked into another room to watch television.

One child, Howard Jr., could bounce a rubber ball against the house for fifteen hours straight. His brother, Edwin, stole anything that wasn't nailed down, and Sissy, who looked like a Hallmark greeting card, was a terrorist from hell.

She would sneak up behind you, dig her nails into your flesh, and then look innocent when her victim cried out in pain.

Howard and Fay usually stayed about five days. One year they had been there nine days when a part went out on their car and they had to send for a new one. The dealership was behind the Iron Curtain.

That night, as I turned carefully in the bunk bed and pulled the *Star Wars* sheets under my chin, I thought about Fay and Howard sprawled out in our queen-size bed and wondered why we did it. Face it. The Semples didn't care about us. We were no more than a stagecoach stop-off, one of the last free meals between their destination and the California freeway. It was eleven o'clock. Howard was still gargling and Howard Jr. was bouncing a rubber ball against the side of the house.

Our guests would spend their mornings watching television while I finished my chores and packed the lunch. In the afternoons, we would do the "tours." This included the malls, the air force museum, and the home of the Wright Brothers. As we pointed proudly to the homestead of the men who brought wings of flight to the world and changed the destiny of man, Howard punched Fay in the arm and said, "Looks like you're going to miss 'As the World Turns' again this afternoon, tootsie."

The goodbyes were always tearful . . . for different reasons. The Semples were about to reenter a world of tipping, paying through the nose for food and lodgings, and doing their own laundry. Little Edwin was about to discover that hotel pictures are bolted to the wall and lamps are screwed to the nightstands. We had tears of joy. We were returning to our own beds.

We had survived another summer with the Semples. But something happened this particular year to change our lives. They had been gone two days when the phone rang. "This is Howard. I hate to call collect, but I'm in a gas station in Barstow, California. Sissy just told us she left her gerbil at your house. It's in a Quaker Oats box with holes in the lid. She left it on the back of the commode in the hallway."

"No problem," I said stiffly.

"The gerbil is pregnant," he continued, "and it's pretty special to Sissy. As a favor, if you could just take care of it and the babies until we drop by on our way home, we'd appreciate it."

As I hung up the phone, something in me snapped. I gathered the family around me and in a shaking voice announced, "The Bombeck Hilton will henceforth be closed during the months of June, July, and August. No more entertaining the parade of visitors who find their way to our driveway. No more housesitting for those around us who see the world and send us postcards reminding us to 'worm the dog' and 'soak the trees.'

"From here on in, we are going to be one of those families who feast at the banquet table of life. We're going to drink in the beauty of majestic mountains, nibble at historical shrines, and stuff ourselves on beaches drenched in solitude. The Bombecks are going to hit the road!

"By all that is holy, I will never host the Semples again!" The family's eyes were frozen on my clenched fist raised above my head. I was clutching the pregnant gerbil.

Closing Down the House

My husband said, "When you're leaving town, it is wise to tell as few people as possible."

I hate it when he talks down to me. What does he think I am? Stupid? The only people I told we were leaving town were:

Tim, our paperboy, who had to tell his branch manager and his sub.

Ralph, our postman, who is not only going to hold our mail, but offered to put a note on the post office bulletin board for someone to cut our grass.

Helen, who has our house key.

My aerobics class and instructor, hairdresser, and dentist.

Closing Down the House

The entire waiting room at the kennel where
  I made arrangements to board the dog.
Marj at the bank, who made out our travel-
  er's checks.
Shirley at AAA, who routed our trip.
The saleswoman who helped me with a
  bathing suit and the nice man who sold me
  a new piece of luggage.
The water softener deliveryman whom I told
  about the key I keep under the white rock
  at the end of the drive.
The dry cleaners . . . in idle conversation.
Sam, our druggist, who prescribed something
  for extreme exposure to sun and children.
The Little League coach and the team.
Evelyn, who was giving a birthday party for
  Stef and needed to know why we weren't
  coming.
The society editor, Marjabelle Mix, who
  wanted a little paragraph for her weekly
  column.

I may not be the most sophisticated traveler
who ever hit the road, but I know enough to sneak
out of town.

Canada

The first time we saw the twenty-two-foot travel trailer, it was parked next to a carport with license plates that had not been renewed in five years. The For Sale sign was flyspecked.

Our entire family encircled it with excitement and wondered what kind of people could part with such a treasure. It was so compact—so self-contained. As my husband and the owner kicked the tires, his wife gave the kids and me a tour of the inside.

The owner worked swiftly. She whipped off the sofa pillows and jammed them into the broom closet, flipped over the table into a bed, and pulled down the bookshelves into a bunk.

"That's amazing," I said. "How does one get into the bunk?"

"You either walk on the face of the person sleeping on the table or boost yourself up by putting your foot on the stove. Make sure the burners are off," she said dryly.

"The kitchen seems rather small." I smiled. "Is there a refrigerator?"

"Of course there's a refrigerator," she said. "Your handbag is covering it. To open the door, everyone but you goes outside. When the door opens, you jump in the sink."

I lingered as she forged ahead to the next section. "Here you have your private quarters." There was a twin bed on either side of the trailer, divided by a small aisle. "There's even a toilet," she added.

"And the door is . . . "

"There isn't any door," she said. "You won't use the toilet anyway. It smells. You'll note there's plenty of room under the beds to store your food, clothes, and blankets. Did you notice the cupboards on the walls? Just tell your husband not to make any sudden stops or everything flies open and you're looking at three days of mopping up."

I fingered a spray nozzle attached to a hose. "How nice. A vegetable brush in the shower."

"That *is* the shower," she said crisply.

I raced to the door, but it was too late. My

husband was shaking hands with the former owner, who held our check.

As we hooked the trailer up to our car, the man pocketed the money and observed, "There goes a piece of our history, Mother. We'll miss it." Her eyes remained dry. "Like the Depression," she said.

Traveling with three kids and dragging a trailer behind us wasn't the swiftest thing we ever did. In retrospect, I should never have given birth to more children than we had car windows. In fact, after a week on the road with them and knowing what I know now, we should have bought a Porsche and rented kids.

"Mom, where are we going again?" the child riding the "hard middle seat" whined. I clutched the steering wheel and stared straight ahead. "Ask your father."

My husband put down the road map. "Don't distract your mother. She's driving. We're going to see one of the most breathtaking phenomena in the world, the Bay of Fundy in New Brunswick, Canada."

"Tell us again why we're going there," queried another bored voice.

"Because you are going to see something that few people have ever seen . . . a bore that comes surging up the Petitcodiac River with a tidal wave that rises to a staggering height of eleven feet at the rate of eight to eleven feet an hour."

"Speaking of tidal waves," said the third voice from the back seat, "I have to go."

"You should have gone before you left home," said their father.

"Dad! That was four days ago. Mom, look for a place to stop."

"I told you before, don't bother your mother. She's got her hands full driving this rig," said my husband.

He got that part right. "Mom" wasn't driving. She was frozen to the steering wheel like she was dragging a tank of nuclear waste material behind her. Every time I looked at the large mirrors on either door, I could see three miles of travel trailers behind me and cars backed up to the United States border.

For the last five hundred miles, I had been following Ruby and Rusty of Kendallville, Indiana, in their RV, True Love. The thought of passing them would have brought on premature menopause.

So far, it hadn't been much of a vacation. Neither of us had anticipated the stress of hauling all this tonnage along the highway. That sweet little couple, Bonnie and Clyde who sold us the travel trailer, never told us the joys of hitting downtown Detroit at five P.M. or the thrill of meeting another car on a bridge designed for a compact and a bicycle. And they certainly never prepared us for the nightly ritual called "parking your home on wheels for the night."

Parking was an exercise for the entire family. My husband needed all the help he could get. He watched the two large mirrors mounted on either door of the car, one child near the rear wheels picked his nose, another at the opposite rear wheel threw rocks at squirrels, and a third child searched for a toilet. It was my job to stand off to one side and coordinate the operation.

"Turn your wheels that way," I shouted.

"Which way? I can't see you. That means nothing to me."

"Left. Turn them left."

"The trailer wheels or the car wheels left?" he shouted.

"Whichever ones make your back wheels straighten out."

"Is that better?"

"Right."

"Is that right as in OK, or right as in turn right? I can't see you in all this rain, you know."

"That's because you didn't listen when I yelled stop. It isn't raining. You just hit the water connection."

"I'm pulling up again. And for God's sake give me better directions. Who are you waving at? Do you want me to go that way?"

"I'm waving to our neighbors."

"Forget the neighbors till we get this parked, then you can get friendly."

"We'd better get friendly now. You just backed into their tent."

It was always a problem. One day in Quebec, it was two o'clock in the afternoon and we had not had lunch because we couldn't find a place to park the trailer . . . something the size of a stadium. In desperation, my husband pulled alongside an abandoned railroad track. After lunch, it was my son's and my turn to put the Barbie and Ken kitchen back in order. The rest of the family took a walk. That's when we heard the train whistle. Both of us froze. It's funny what you think about when your last seconds on earth are imminent. You don't do any of the things you're supposed to do like grab the picture albums or fall to your knees and confess your sins. All I could think about was those women on the *Titanic* who had refused dessert the night the ship hit an iceberg because their clothes felt tight. As my son hummed "Nearer My God to Thee," I stuffed a Twinkie in my mouth as the train roared by. Every dish in the trailer crashed to the floor.

My mind drifted back to the True Love, and I wondered if Rusty and Ruby of Kendallville, Indiana, were having a good time. You get to know a lot about people you have been following for five hundred miles. I knew they had a Baby on Board, had been to Williamsburg and Knotts Berry Farm, and were members of the

NRA. They liked the open road and had a bumper sticker that read CAMPERS ARE THE MOST HONEST PEOPLE IN THE WORLD. (They also had a lock on their gas tank.)

Somehow, I knew that Rusty was driving and Ruby was reading a road map to her husband who "knew damn well he was going east and if the sun was setting there, then God had made a mistake!" Rusty was crabby because he couldn't find a holding station to empty the waste and they couldn't use their self-contained toilet. Ruby worried about the brakes burning out when they went downhill. Her life had no meaning without a laundromat. The big saucepan she used to cook spaghetti in now held bait. Their kids ordered $10 dinners in restaurants and ate only the pickle. Their dog got carsick and rode with his head out of the window with his fanny in Ruby's face.

My husband put down the road map again. "We've only made ten miles today. No wonder. Look who you're following. It's Rusty and Ruby again. Pass him. He's only going thirty-five miles per hour."

"We're going uphill," I said. "I don't have the power."

As we descended, Rusty sped up to sixty-five miles per hour. He was incredible when you thought about it. He never stopped for scenic views. Never got gas. He had to have kidneys the size of basketballs. If he didn't pick it up, we'd never get to the Bay of Fundy.

All told, the trip would take a month. It would take us through the breathtaking forests of Ontario, where our evenings would be spent watching bears eat food in the dump. We would inch our way through the narrow cobblestone streets of Quebec and wind along the St. Lawrence River, around the snakelike coast of the Gaspé. On Prince Edward Island, we would scour the beaches for clams, and in Nova Scotia we would sit on the grass and listen to bagpipe concerts.

Well, some of us would. Others of us would carry water, build fires, hustle garbage, and spend most of our waking hours in a laundromat. While the family was pretending they were throwbacks from a wagon train, I spent most of my time scrounging for quarters and watching my enzymes and bleach race their way to the dirt and grime in our underwear.

The camping experience turned out to be as joyous as giving birth. Each day brought new challenges and tests of our tolerance for one another. But no matter how many flat tires we changed, how many repairs we needed for things that leaked and boiled over, no matter how many times I was tempted to make a necklace out of

Valium and lick at them all day long, our goal always sustained us. We were going to see the great tidal bore at the Bay of Fundy. No one in our neighborhood had seen anything like that!

We arrived in the small town of Moncton in New Brunswick in the early afternoon and drove our travel trailer to the banks of the Petitcodiac River. My husband turned his attention to his camera, mounting it carefully on a tripod and trying out different locations. I passed out slickers to the children with orders to stand back at a safe distance and hold Mommy's hand tightly lest they be sucked into the jaws of the powerful waters.

At around 3:05, the buzz of anticipation by the spectators became hushed. There was an eerie silence as binoculars were trained on the flow of rolling water in the distance.

We strained our ears to hear the roar of rushing waves we knew would soon come crashing against the shore. Our eyes searched to glimpse the wild wall of force that would leave us wet and breathless.

At 3:10, a small trickle of brown water, barely visible, slowly edged its way down the river toward us with all the excitement of a stopped-up toilet. The five of us stared silently as the dribble lazily lapped the shore like a kitten with warm milk. I retained more water than that. The crowd was underwhelmed and stood staring like statues. It was a long time before anyone in our family spoke. About five thousand miles to be exact.

In the fall, the kids used the travel trailer to entertain sleepovers. But for the most part, after the Canadian trip, it occupied a space between the garbage cans and the garage. The For Sale sign in the rear window was as aggressive as we got.

One day that winter, a young serviceman and his wife knocked at the door and asked to see it. He was stationed nearby and needed low-cost housing they could park near the base. As our husbands kicked the tires, I showed the young bride the inside of the trailer. When I finished, she said quietly, "The sink seems rather small."

"Not really," I said. "It seats one real comfortably."

"How do you know that?" she asked.

"Do you use the refrigerator a lot?"

She hesitated. "Not a whole lot."

"Then it isn't important." I smiled.

By the time she rushed to her husband's side, it was too late. The check was in my husband's hand.

During the rest of that winter, I thought a lot about our first attempt at "quality time." Was it possible there were vacations where you didn't have to carry your own toilet paper and dispose of your own waste? Somewhere was there a wonderland where nightlife was more than a ranger picking his teeth with a matchbook cover and showing slides of "The Birth of a Bog"?

Some of our friends had actually gone on trips where they didn't have to cut up everyone's meat or listen to a car radio that made their teeth swell. They visited a world where crying children belonged to someone else, and when they stretched out their arms on the back seat to relax, someone didn't put wads of chewing gum in their hands.

That's the world I wanted to explore.

"Honey, I Just Ditched the Kids"

When my children get their own literary agent (and it is only a matter of time), the first chapter in their Dearest book will record this moment in great detail.

They will describe how they sat on the edge of the bed watching Mommy and Daddy pack for a twenty-one-day European Getaway.

As they fight back tears of rejection, they will reflect on how they were left behind with nothing but $5,000 worth of toys, a $2,000 entertainment center, enough soft drinks to launch the *QE2*, color-coordinated menus, and an overpriced babysitter who would hover over them like security in a Loehmann's dressing room. They will tell of how their mother traveled twelve thousand miles with a blowfish balanced between her knees to buy their affection back. Their book will inspire tabloid headlines: MY DAD WAS TOO BUSY TO BOND.

The big question that should be addressed here is not whether parents should take their children on vacation or leave them at home. The question is, What is the best age to leave them behind?

The answer is, The younger the better. People who think teenagers can be responsible enough to be left alone are in for a shock.

Realistically, a three-year-old does not put eight hundred miles on your car in a week and pour diet cola in the radiator when it boils over. A three-year-old does not summon one hundred of her closest friends to a party before your plane takes off. An infant will not use "emergency funds" to replace the sliding glass door that someone sailed a chair through.

Parents who have never before left their children for any length of time anguish for weeks about the time they will spend away from their kids. They will torture themselves with the thought of those little cherub faces waking up in the middle of the night calling, "Mommy! Daddy!"

They will punish themselves with the memory of those tearful reflections pressed against the window waving bye-bye as they pull out of the driveway.

This feeling will last ten . . . fifteen minutes tops.

Packing

One never realizes how different a husband and wife can be until they begin to pack for a trip. My husband has obviously never heard of the old axiom for travelers, "Pack half the clothes you planned to take and twice the money."

His bed is covered with apparel.

If someone should "just happen" to award him the Nobel Peace Prize, he has the clothes for it.

He has the wardrobe to parachute behind enemy lines dressed as a mercenary and clothes to commandeer a torpedo boat through a squall.

If there is a bar mitzvah, ten-kilometer run, costume party, fire in the hotel, bowling tournament, western cookout, or rain for forty days and forty nights, he's ready.

He can attend an underwater wedding or a mountain hike, change a tire or christen a ship.

He has clothes to barter for mules and guides in a Colombian jungle as well as outfits for snorkeling, safaris, high teas, low ceilings; clothes for lounging and clothes to leave behind as tips.

He has an iron that weighs thirteen ounces and folds into the size of a ballpoint pen, a hair dryer, and a global clock that tells you the time where you're not. (He will never have the right voltage to use any of these items.)

He has a personal coffeepot, cassette player, and gym bag full of language cassettes. He carries Tom Clancy's latest eight-hundred-page hardcover novel, a pair of binoculars, a calculator that figures out what the U.S. dollar translates to, lead-laminated pouches to protect his film, a Swiss army knife, and several rolls of toilet tissue. He covers each of his shoes in a little bag as if he is gift-wrapping it.

Off to one side is his food stash. These are little boxes and packets in separate bags that he clings to like diplomatic pouches that he never lets out of his sight. There's a supply of granola, crackers, dried soups, fruits, beef jerky, snacks, and candy bars. I don't know how to tell him London is not a third-world city.

I, on the other hand, have benefited from the advice of Sylvia Suitcase (probably not her real name), a packing expert who appeared one day on Sally Jessy Raphael. Sylvia said if you really planned carefully you could make one hundred and thirty-five combinations out of a twelve-piece wardrobe and be well-dressed for three weeks.

Stacked neatly on my bed is my ensemble: a basic dress, reversible skirt, slacks, blouse, jacket, shorts, T-shirt, vest, two scarves, cap with a bill, and jumpsuit for airline travel, plus underwear and a few toiletries.

When my husband's luggage is stacked by the door it will look like the road company of *Les Miserables*. Just before I zipped my single overnighter suitcase, he said to me, "By the way, do you have room for my tripod?" For those of you who think pictures grow on postcards, I will explain that a tripod is a three-legged stand that supports a camera so it will remain perfectly still. When fully extended, a tripod will stand waist-high and weigh in at two or three pounds.

Men with tripods will tell you how they were able to capture a hummingbird with crossed eyes or a cloud over the Kremlin that looked like the ghost of Billy Crystal, but they won't tell you their tripod was in their room at the time.

"What do you need a tripod for?" I ask patiently.

"Just in case I want to keep my camera steady while I take a spectacular shot of the Alps or something."

"You borrowed an Instamatic camera from my

father that fits in your shirt pocket. What's to steady?" I ask.

I know better than to argue. I jam the tripod on top of my twelve-piece basic ensemble that can make one hundred and thirty-five combinations and keep me well-dressed for three weeks.

I snap my suitcase shut, lock it, and sit down on the bed to wait.

We are scheduled to leave for Europe in two weeks.

Twenty-One-Day European Getaway

I said it was our ninth country and our four-teenth continental breakfast. My husband said I was wrong. It was our fifth country and our twelfth continental breakfast.

I waved the itinerary under his nose as our bus sped along the autobahn in Germany. We had been snapping at one another since Amsterdam—or was it Austria?—and we didn't know why. I blamed our surliness on the continental breakfasts. There was no doubt in my mind that it caused mood swings and possible genetic side effects. Since day one, the morning meal had not varied once. It consisted of a paper napkin, a knife, a fork and spoon for which we had no use, a cup and saucer, canned fruit juice, a pot of coffee or tea, and a container of marmalade. There was, of course, the proverbial hard roll.

For the first few days of our nine-country, twenty-one-day European Getaway, there were smiles from the group when the continental breakfasts were put before them. Women pinched their waists and said, "This is what I need. I promised myself I wouldn't pig out." By the end of the first week, no one spoke when the basket of hard rolls was placed on the table. We all knew the truth. The continental breakfast is not designed to make you thin. Even if it is eaten in small pieces, it will expand and distribute itself on your hips and thighs until you are molded into its image. My husband accused the tour company of issuing the same rolls every morning. He said they scooped up the uneaten ones and forwarded them to our next destination. I told him he was being ridiculous, but he was adamant. He carved his initials and the date in a hard roll in Dublin and said he would prove his point when we got to Paris.

We knew the trip was structured when we signed on for it. After all, wasn't that the point? We were neophyte travelers who had never been out of the country before. We would see as much as we possibly could in a limited amount of time. The death march was a trade-off for the benefits of having someone take care of us, tell us what to eat and when, direct us where to go and when to leave, interpret what was being said, tell us when our luggage was missing, and protect us from all those foreigners staring at us from the other side of the bus's tinted glass.

As the bus picked up speed, the exit sign loomed majestically to our left, and everyone on the bus rolled their eyes, knowing what was to come. The German word for exit is *Ausfahrt* and every time we saw it, you could count on eighty-seven-year-old Mr. Fleck to say the same thing, "My mother doesn't allow me to use words like that." I wanted to shout that his mother probably swam out to meet troop ships in the Crimean War, but my husband put his hand across my mouth and whispered, "It's the hard rolls talking."

The thing about tours is that it doesn't take long to size up your fellow passengers and label them. They are as stereotypical as characters out of an English mystery. The reason you get to know them so well is that the same group shows up on every guided tour you will ever take. Their faces and names will change, but the personalities are an integral part of tour travel.

Riding in the front seat (always!) is the tour's Health Fairy. She's a retired English teacher from Boston who keeps a daily log on who is irregular and who "got back on track" during the night. Every morning there is a report on who has bacterial problems and where they got them. She speaks fluent pharmacy and carries a handbag the size of a dispensary. If you have swollen ankles, sore throat, motion sickness, poor circulation, constipation, burning eyes, or PMS, she's there for you.

Seated just behind her is "Where's Mr. Babcock?" He is traveling alone. No one knows his first name. "Where's Mr. Babcock?" is all we ever hear. He has three cameras around his neck, a vest jammed full of film, a gym bag crammed with light meters, and a portable tripod. Every time we pass a tree, "Where's Mr. Babcock?" jumps out of his seat and asks the driver to stop so he can get a shot. When the bus makes a regular stop for "photo opportunities," count on "Where's Mr. Babcock?" to hold up the entire tour before he reboards. In Garmisch, he shot three rolls of Ektachrome of a dog with one ear up.

Two days ago, when "Where's Mr. Babcock?" defied the guide's instructions to line up to see Hadrian's Wall and later remained behind to photograph a man relieving himself on it, we voted on whether to leave him there. It was real close.

Ben and his wife, Has-Ben Everywhere, are a couple from New Jersey. They have matched

French luggage, and they informed everyone on their first day that they do not generally go on tours but arrange to have their own car and driver. They do not socialize a lot with the other group members. The only time they talk is to mention it's too bad we couldn't have "done Europe" when it was elegant. When they were there years ago, Venus de Milo had arms. No matter what you buy, they bought the same thing ten years ago for a fraction of what you paid.

Everyone tries to stay out of the path of Joan and Bud Whiner. Excuse the pun, they're a pair-of-noids to draw to. Every morning we are treated to their litany of complaints. "Well, they gave us the servants' quarters again" is a staple. The food is inedible, the service unacceptable, and the tour company is going to hear from them. In Rome, they felt the church tour was tilted in favor of Catholic churches.

I cannot say Mr. Murchison's name without whispering it. Everyone else does. When the group rendezvoused in New York, he had taken a few belts to "relax." We never saw him tense. He is "over-served" in every country we visit. Somehow, he can't be categorized as an "ugly American." You have to be conscious to be that. He simply is seeing Europe through the bottom of a Jack Daniels bottle. If he would remain quiet, we could put a handle in his mouth and check him through as another piece of luggage. But Mr. Murchison likes to sing when he's had a few drinks. In Limerick, Ireland, he stood up in the Cathedral of St. Mary and sang "When Irish Eyes Are Smiling." In Amsterdam, when we toured the red-light district where the prostitutes sit in store windows on chairs, he warbled "How Much Is That Doggie in the Window?" In Venice, he nearly fell into the canal singing "O Sole Mio."

He didn't sing in Lucerne. However, he did put his cigarette out in the fondue.

The couple I like are Mary Jo and her mother, Lil. Like us, it's their first trip out of the country and they're thrilled with everything they see. When Lil saw her "first Irish dog," she could barely speak. Mary Jo is keeping a diary right down to the menus.

In the back of the bus are the poor Jacksons. They don't have first names either. They're a couple from Oklahoma who are being followed by their luggage across Europe. But not close enough. They have been wearing the same clothes for seventeen days.

I relate to the Jacksons. That stupid jumpsuit that Sylvia Suitcase recommended is so stiff from wearing, it could walk to Rome by itself. Not only that, I discovered you have to have the talents of a stripper to wear it.

On a plane en route from New York to

London, I was in the restroom when the captain announced we were experiencing turbulence and should return to our seats. Before I could get it all together, my jumpsuit dropped to thirty-two thousand feet in a pool of water while my body leveled off at thirty-four-thousand feet. When I finally emerged from the bathroom, my husband observed, "You don't look good enough to have been in there that long."

"Don't start with me," I said. "I just dropped my belt down the commode."

"What's the red mark on your forehead?"

"I hit it on the doorknob."

"What were you doing down there?"

"You wouldn't believe it if I told you."

There should be a label in jumpsuits that shows a glass of water with an X through it.

Actually, the bus ride in between the touring is rather relaxing. There is a myth that guided tours are a piece of cake—nothing to do but wait for your travel guide to count the luggage, open doors for you, and pass out tickets to your next adventure. That's not true. We have a lot to do.

To begin with, we have to remember our bus number. On a twenty-one-day tour, you could average thirty-five buses, each from a different country and each with a different driver. If you are in Germany, the bus driver will be Asian. If you are in Spain, the driver will be Russian. If you are touring France with a French driver, you are on the wrong bus.

Today, we are on a German bus with an Italian driver. He is the first foreigner we've seen close up since we left home. Mary Jo got his autograph and picture. His English is spoken like a recording. "My name is Luigi," he says into a microphone that is inches from his teeth. "Remember that and remember your bus number. It is 1084725. Keep your feet out of the aisles, do not smoke, do not leave valuables on the bus, keep the windows closed, have the correct change for the restrooms, do not bring food aboard, and remember, if you miss your bus, you must return to your hotel at your own expense. If you have a good time, you may tip as you leave."

Remembering your guide is also taxing. You cannot drift for a minute. Although Mr. Duval is our main guide, we pick up local ones to provide information on what we are seeing. The women guides usually carry umbrellas, plastic flowers, or brightly colored scarfs so we can follow them easily. Male guides try to lose us.

Mr. Duval announces every evening that we must have our luggage outside our hotel doors by five A.M. Never at nine or ten, but at a time when we are asleep. Sometimes, as I drag it out into the hall, my husband's hand is still in his valise attached to clean underwear.

This sounds ludicrous, but if it weren't for

Mary Jo and her copious notes, no one would know what country we're in.

As the bus slows down, the Whiners peer anxiously out of the window. "I knew it," says Bud, "another factory. We didn't pay all of this money to come to a bunch of tourist traps."

I hated to admit it, but Bud had a point. Our sightseeing did seem to be a bit out of balance. We were allowed fifteen minutes to view the Book of Kells in Ireland and an hour and a half to shop in a sweater factory. We spent twenty minutes touring the Tower of London and two hours in an English bone china factory. We saw Anne Frank's house when the bus slowed down but spent half a day in Holland's Delft factory. Add to that the jewelry factory in Austria, the Murano glass factory in Italy, the lace factory in Belgium, and the watch factory in Switzerland, and we were pretty burned out.

This was a wood carving factory. We all filed off the bus to Luigi's warning, "Remember, your bus number is 1084725. Take your time."

The factories are all the same. There is a small room the size of a coffee table where an artisan sits on a stool with the product in front of him. This craftsman was chipping away on a bust of Elvis. A guide quickly explains the process. Seconds later, we are herded through two double doors to a room the size of Connecticut. Every three feet along the rows of glass counters displaying hand-carved dogs and tableaus of the Crucifixion is a salesperson with an order book who speaks English like a Harvard professor.

Having never traveled extensively before, I was surprised at how many cathedrals we could visit in one day. The first church we toured was truly a spiritual experience. As I shuffled down the aisle and gawked toward the ceiling, I clung hungrily to every word about the church that came from the guide's lips. Then when I could absorb no more, I wrote it all down in a notebook. I was desperate to know how long it took to build it, how many bricks were used, what year it was struck by lightning, when the east wing was added, the time it took to install the organ, how many trees were cut down to make the pews, how many men died cutting the trees, how many gallons of gold leaf were used on the ceiling alone, and how many miles of scaffolding were needed to restore it. I duly recorded what heads of state were buried from there and in what city the bells were cast. I think one day I actually pushed "Where's Mr. Babcock?" into a water font to get closer to the guide.

After forty or fifty cathedrals, I began to glaze over and became quite preoccupied. When souvenir church bulletins were passed out in a basilica somewhere, I wrapped my gum in mine. Later, when the guide asked, "Any questions?" I asked how many cathedrals could you see in one day before you slipped into a coma.

Near the end of the trip, St. Paul's began to look like St. John Lateran and Santa Maria Maggiore looked suspiciously like St. Mark's. I began noticing saints with bad skin, chipped noses, and missing fingers. I really began to worry about myself when I nudged my husband, nodded toward a statue of St. Cecelia, and said, "Be honest. Is that Lee Marvin's twin or what!"

Eventually, it got to the point where it would have taken Robert Redford saying Mass to get me off the bus.

As the death march progressed, other things began to bother me. My twelve-piece basic ensemble that could make a hundred thirty-five combinations was beginning to break down. The breast pocket on the jacket ripped and I could only wear it with my arms folded. A scarf faded on my only blouse, forcing me to wear it with the darts facing backwards. The T-shirt shrunk. I bought another cap with a bill and made an interesting bra to wear around the pool.

I had outgrown my slacks in London . . . or was it Rome?

We were all getting testy. The moment my husband hit a hotel room, he unpacked like we had just closed on escrow for the building. Every suitcase was emptied into drawers and closets . . . if only for a night. Then he began his laundry. The sun could be setting over the Matterhorn. A carnival could fill the streets of Florence. The Tour de France winner could be coming over the finish line outside our hotel window. He did his laundry.

I was also sick of lugging around his stupid tripod. A perfect stranger approached me one day in Harrods, pointed to the permanent indentation on my jumpsuit, and said, "I see you travel with a tripod."

Probably the biggest downside to group tour travel is that for twenty-one days, sixteen hours a day, you are with other Americans. God forbid you should rub shoulders with an Austrian, German, Frenchman, Swiss, Italian, Irishman, Belgian, Englishman, or Dutchman. You wait in hotel lobbies with groups of other Americans waiting for their tour buses. You visit shrines where all the buses that unload are carrying other Americans. You eat with one another at long tables that cater to Americans and are sequestered in private dining rooms like juries.

Guides tell you American jokes in English. You are dropped off at souvenir shops that sell T-shirts with the Chicago Bulls stamped on them. When you go to a circus or the theater, you are set off in a section reserved for American tourists. In three weeks, the closest we ever got to a foreigner was Lil's Irish dog.

The bus rolled on and the twenty-first day found us gathered on the second terrace of the world-famous Eiffel Tower for the obligatory gala farewell party.

I looked at this group of people whom I had seen more often than my mother and had more intimacy with than my gynecologist. We had shared some extraordinary moments together.

We had dined in a castle at a medieval banquet in Ireland. (Ben Everywhere observed the Samoun Fumme was cold and Wortes-Sallet-Ton-Tressis was tougher than he remembered.)

We had seen the Pope standing in his window waving from St. Peter's Square. (The Whiners said they didn't believe it was really him. They saw someone push a start button in his back.)

Mary Jo and her mother had yodeled on stage at the Swiss Night Out party in Lucerne. We had been to the London Palladium and the Sistine Chapel.

As we sipped the complimentary French wine, my husband started to butter his hard roll. Suddenly he jumped to his feet and dramatically hoisted the roll over his head like Kunta Kinte offering up his newborn son. "I knew it!" he shouted. "It's my roll from Dublin. Here are my initials and the date!"

The Whiners said they weren't surprised.

The Everywheres looked bored and told him to sit down.

"Where's Mr. Babcock?" blinded him with his flash as he captured the moment on film.

Mary Jo and her mother declared it a miracle.

Mr. Murchison offered a toast and a fast chorus of "Mademoiselle from Armentieres, Parlez Vous."

The Health Fairy warned, "Don't eat it. It will make you gassy."

When we arrived home, I set fire to my travel clothes. To me, they had the same symbolism as maternity clothes. Get rid of them and you would never have to go through the experience again.

The tour was a nice smorgasbord of Europe, but we felt constricted by time schedules and bound by an itinerary where people hovered over you as if you were an endangered species during mating season.

After the guided tour experience, we fantasized about renting a car and taking off all by ourselves. In our dreams, we imagined the two of us immersed in a little red sports car like two lovers in a hot tub. We visualized the wind blowing our hair as we discovered quaint little inns on dirt roads. We paused on a mountaintop to drink wine and toast the breathless view.

"We could set our own pace," I said to my husband. "No stress . . . no tour buses . . . no guides."

"You're right," he said.

"No luggage outside the room by five A.M., no

table for twenty at lunch, no more major decisions of 'Do I use my fifteen minutes to tour the Louvre or go to the restroom'"

In retrospect, it sounded so simple. If you could drive a car, you could drive a rental car in another country, right?

Right.

The Rental Car

We were stopped for a traffic light at the mall one afternoon when one of our kids noted that the car in front of us had his windshield wipers on even though the sun was shining. He was also trying to make a left-hand turn from the center lane.

"Is he crazy or what?" giggled my son.

I grabbed the kid by the collar and put my face close to his. "Listen up, mister! I never want to hear you use that tone again, do you understand me? Look at the plates. That poor unfortunate that you have deemed to call crazy is driving a rental car. Do you know what that means? It means he has a road map that looks like the veins in the back of my knees and he was lucky to find his way out of the airport. He is in a car that he has never seen before and is looking for his route signs that are hidden somewhere behind a tree. There are fifteen pieces of luggage jammed into that compact because they didn't have the station wagon he ordered. The poor devil will never find out how to turn on the lights when it gets dark so he will have to drive until his battery dies. If he's real lucky, he will find the button that releases the key in his ignition. If he doesn't he will have to spend the night in the car. Don't you ever talk that way about a person driving a rental car again!"

My son looked at me and said softly, "It's Italy again, isn't it, Mom?"

Italy

The Italian behind the car rental desk in Naples boredly drew a circle around a large X and said, "You are here." Then he outlined an artery on the map with a yellow pen and continued, "Just turn right at the first—"

"We're where?" asked my husband, leaning over for a closer look.

"Here," he repeated, stabbing the map with his pen.

"But 'here' is in the margin," I interrupted. "How do we get onto the map?"

"It is simple, madam." He sighed. "Take the Via Don to Foria and follow the Piazza Cavour to Via Roma. Look for the Piazza Medaglia d'Oro off Via Giotto Menzinger and follow the signs. You can't miss it."

It had all sounded so romantic. We'd pop over to Italy, rent a car, and wind around the Amalfi Drive, taking in Positano and Ravello and perhaps zip over to Capri. We certainly didn't need a guide for that!

Besides, driving in Italy wouldn't be like driving in Ireland. That had been a nightmare. From the moment my husband eased himself into the driver's seat at Shannon, he sensed something was wrong. "Where's my steering wheel?" he asked.

"I've got it," I said. "It's on my side."

Carefully, he eased his body over the gearshift and into the seat. He started the motor and inched his way onto the highway where he nearly met another car head on. After two more close calls, we realized everyone was driving his car on the *wrong* (left) side of the road. I'm here to tell you we have lived life in the fast lane and life in the slow lane, but until you've spent a few weeks in the wrong lane, you have nothing to talk about.

It was terrifying for my husband. Every time a car approached, he came to a dead stop and closed his eyes until it passed. When he tried to turn on the lights, he released the hood. When he thought he was shifting gears with his right hand, he opened his own door. When he attempted to enter a lane of traffic, he looked for traffic the wrong way. In the entire two weeks we toured the country, we never passed another car, never put the car in reverse, never parallel parked or made a left-hand turn . . . make that right-hand turn.

As a passenger, it was no day at the beach for me either. Each time we passed a person walking, I sucked in my breath and made a whimpering noise. When my husband asked me not to do that, I informed him I had been flogged to death by tree branches, drenched by gutter and curb water, mooned by sheep, and seen fear in the eyes of pedestrians that would haunt me for the rest of my life.

For months after we returned home from Ireland, I had nightmares about the "round-abouts"—the Irish's answer to a samurai clover-leaf. No wonder the country boasts such religious fervor. There are probably more instant conversions to the faith on a roundabout than on death row.

What it is is a circle with four lanes of traffic going in the same direction, with six or seven exits and entrances feeding into it. Once you enter the roundabout, cars zip in and out in front of you at blurring speeds. Everyone in the car takes a vow of silence while you are entering and exiting the roundabout. We once spent a half day on one.

Before leaving the Italian car rental counter, I asked, "Italians do drive on the right side of the road, don't they?" For the first time, the agent smiled and said, "Of course. You will have no problem in Naples. Just be sure to put all your belongings in the trunk and out of sight, including your handbag. Scoundrels, you know."

It was not the first time we had heard of crime in some of the larger European cities. Handbags were reportedly ripped from your shoulders by "scoundrels" on motor scooters. Gypsy "scoundrel" children surrounded you as you walked. When they disappeared, your wallet and valuables went with them. There was talk that windows on your car were smashed as you stopped for a traffic light and your luggage was rerouted.

We made a vow to be careful.

The two-seater sports car we had ordered turned out to be a station wagon that was less than user-friendly. The motor didn't purr. It made human sounds in Italian. When you slammed the door, the radio went on. The reverse gear was one of the best-kept secrets since the formula for rocket fuel. Once the key was inserted in the ignition, there was no way to remove it. We circled the airport for thirty minutes before we finally stumbled onto the Via Don.

To tell you how long it took us to find our hotel would have no meaning for anyone in hours. As a frame of reference, I will simply tell you that Susan Butcher covered 1,158 miles from Anchorage to Nome in eleven days, one hour, fifty-three minutes, and twenty-three seconds to win the Iditarod. She was in deep snow and freezing conditions on a sled being pulled by a team of dogs at the time.

It took us five hours and thirty-three minutes to cover twenty miles to our hotel in a Fiat.

Naples traffic isn't a condition. It's a war in progress. There are eight to ten lanes of traffic all going on an accelerated treadmill to oblivion. Red lights flash, but no one stops. Green lights flash, but no one cares. Cars cut in and out in front of you and never exit anywhere. New ones just keep feeding into the traffic. The street signs are all in (what else?) Italian, straining to the limits my entire Italian vocabulary, which consists of "antipasto" and "Joe Garagiola."

"How do those people survive as pedestrians?" I asked my husband.

"They were born right there on the sidewalk," he snarled.

As darkness approached and we were still driving around Naples, panic set in. Soon we would have to turn on the car lights, and then what would we do? We were afraid to touch anything in the car. We might even be faced with running out of gas. In that traffic, how long would it be before someone even noticed we weren't moving under our own steam, but were being pushed along with the traffic? One year? Two?

As we sped down the wrong way on a one-way street, a bus approached. My husband swerved off into a dark alley to miss getting hit head-on. We sat there for a moment in the darkness before my husband noticed a glow of a dozen or so cigarettes behind the car. They belonged to a group of young men leaning on motorcycles. In my heart I knew they had "scoundrel" written all over their bodies.

Angrily, my husband opened his door and said, "I'm going to tell them we're tourists and we're lost."

I grabbed his arm. "No matter what the outcome of this evening is," I said, "I just wanted you to know that this is the stupidest thing you have ever done in your entire life."

"Look," he said, "I don't care if they're Peter Fonda and Dennis Hopper. We've got to find the hotel."

After a few minutes of conversation, one of the young men climbed into the front seat of the car with my husband. I was told to get in the rear seat. Another young man climbed on his bike and motioned for us to follow. Together, they delivered us to the doors of our hotel. When we tried to pay them, they refused and told us to have a nice stay in Naples . . . and be careful with our cameras and handbags. There were scoundrels about.

I tell this story for two reasons. First, because it's the kind of story you never hear about—the nice people on your travels who are glad you have come to their country and want to show it off. Second, it marks the only time I can remember that my husband admitted to being lost.

By the time we crawled into bed that night, we knew what we had to do. We were going to put our rental car in a garage somewhere and hire a driver to take us to Pompeii and Mount Vesuvius.

That's when we met Frank. Frank was a concierge at the hotel who had a way of conducting business with you and painting the lobby with his eyes at the same time. We asked him if he knew of a driver who would not only be knowledgeable, but who spoke English.

Frank shrugged. "No problem. I get you good driver who speaks English better than you do." Frank made a phone call. We tipped him.

If Henry Kissinger had been Italian and had a lip full of Novocain, he would have sounded like the driver Frank got for us. His name was Rocco. We asked Rocco if he had been called often by Frank to serve as a guide/driver for English-speaking tourists. He said, "Oh sure, he's my brother."

We had the feeling when we tipped Rocco, we tipped Frank again.

Someone told us that Naples has the best pizza in the world. Where do you find the best pizza in Naples? You silly goose. You ask Frank. Frank said, "No problem," he would make reservations for us that night. He made a phone call. We tipped him.

Later that night as we walked into the restaurant, a familiar face approached us with the menus. It was Frank. He owned the restaurant and worked there on his nights off from the hotel. We left a tip for the pizza *and* Frank.

We were to discover in the next few days that Frank had relatives who ran "best jewelry factory in Naples" and a brother-in-law with "best laundry" in all of Italy. I knew in my heart that in a few years, Frank would have enough in tips for a down payment on his own country.

Watching state-of-the-art nepotism was fun, but we had to push on to the drive down the Amalfi coast. Both of us were apprehensive as we stared at the rented Fiat sitting at the curb.

"Is it pointed in the direction of the autostrada?" asked my husband. (The autostrada is the Italian version of an expressway.)

"No problem," said Frank. "You go down and make a left and at the first turnoff a right and you are there. Then you get off at Amalfi exit."

We tipped him.

We couldn't believe that something had worked out right. The autostrada was exactly where Frank said it would be. We stopped at the toll booth, gave them a chunk of lire, and watched for our exit. When we arrived at the toll booth at the other end, it was obvious we had overshot the Amalfi exit, so we paid another chunk of lire to get back on and go the other way.

When we once again reached our original toll booth, we realized we had missed it again. My husband said maybe you could only exit going one way, so we paid another toll and got back on.

At the other end as we forked out our fourth toll, I said, "This is ridiculous; I'm going to ask."

"Don't be silly," he said. "It's here. We're just not seeing it. Pay attention this time."

I yelled out of the window, "Where's the Amalfi exit?"

The man in the toll booth yelled back, "It's called Maiori!"

In Positano as we stopped for a light, a large group of tourists walked in front of us to board their tour bus. One of them yelled at my husband, "Your windshield wipers are on."

"I know," shouted my husband. "I'm making a left-hand turn." The man stared at us for a minute and then walked on.

"I thought you released your hood when you wanted to turn left," I said.

"I release the hood when I want to turn right."

I looked over my shoulder as the group boarded their tour bus—and was filled with envy.

Tipping

Tipping has become as mechanical to Americans as swatting a fly buzzing around the potato salad. Foreigners tell us we are responsible for the decadent bit of capitalism that turns Boy Scouts into money-grubbing urchins. They contend many countries with people pledged to give good service on the basis of pride have been corrupted by the American dollar. This is probably true.

I remember one New Year's Eve we hired a babysitter to watch our children. The teenager invited in a few friends for a party, broke a gin bottle in our fireplace, burned a hole in the family room rug, locked the kids in their rooms, and threw up on our sofa, which had to be re-covered at some expense.

My husband tipped her five dollars because it was New Year's Eve and she had stayed after midnight.

It's a habit we cannot leave home without.

We have tipped waiters who removed a cat from the table where we were eating. We have tipped cabdrivers who nearly orphaned our children. We have rewarded curbside porters for holding our luggage at the curb as our plane took off.

Americans do pay for the strangest services. During the years I have been traveling, I have paid possibly $700 (and that's a conservative figure) to get back my garment bag that originally cost $60. On the occasions that I wanted to carry it myself, it was literally ripped from my hands. Unfortunately, the IRS does not consider this garment bag a dependent. It should.

In one trip alone, I paid to have it checked in at curbside, rescued from the top of a carousel by a skycap, put into the trunk of a waiting cab, picked up by a hotel bellman who dropped it into the hands of another bellman who finally deposited it in my room. At this point, I invested more in tips than the contents of the bag were worth. Small wonder President Carter carried his own luggage.

In some places, tipping is a major industry. Take Haiti. If you plan to ride a mule to the mountaintop fortress of Henri Christophe's Citadel, you will never be lonely.

There are twenty or thirty mules at the bottom of the historic climb for tourists. There are also three hundred unemployed children ready to help the tourists. There is a child to assist you in getting on the mule, another child to put his hand on the left side of the reins, and another to put his hand on the right side of the reins. There is another optimistic child who places his hand on your buttock to keep you from falling off the mule and another one with a switch who whacks the mule when it pauses to pass out. This quintet of children will stick to you like ugly wallpaper for the entire trip up and down the mountain and will not leave you until you reward them for their vigil. If you are carrying a camera bag, purse, and raincoat, prepare to hire an accountant to handle the payroll.

As far as I'm concerned, tipping comes with the territory. How can I complain when I used to give my kids an allowance for breathing? It's the American way. In Las Vegas, tipping is state of the art. Never have so few done so little and gotten so much. One night we went to a casino showroom to see "Frank" and bought our tickets. The tickets got us inside the door. No farther. A man in a black tuxedo surveyed the empty room and said, "There is nothing any closer." My husband gave him five dollars and his vision improved. He spotted a table six feet from where we were standing.

I still couldn't make out the stage. I looked at the second maitre d' and told him I had sold blood to get here. His expression never changed. My husband tipped him and we passed on to the third maitre d' another six feet away.

This went on for fifteen minutes. Thirty dollars later, we were seated at a long table straight out of a VFW lodge. To view the stage we had to turn our heads into a locked position for one hour. Frank sat on a crummy stool. I figured he didn't tip.

It is reasonable to recognize good service, but one practice in most foreign countries is unforgivable. You must pay for the privilege of using a restroom *before* you set foot in it. I'm pushing for the Worldwide Freedom Potty Act that should be a part of the Geneva Convention, the Treaty of Versailles, and all those documents that grant everyone the right of a facility when the need arises.

"Surely," I told my husband, "there is someplace where you can go without wearing a money changer around your waist . . . a Shangri-la where smiles come easily . . . a magical place where people pamper and hover over you because they just want you to be happy."

Cruising the Baltic

It was another one of those predictable evenings. By eight-thirty we were in our nightclothes, semiprone in our matching Barcalounger recliners, watching animals mate on PBS.

As we were searching for a special on "The Monogamous Manatee," the screen filled with Kathie Lee Gifford bopping around a cruise ship singing, "Eatin' what you want and doin' what you choose." Everyone around her was half sick from happiness.

My husband observed, "Look at that! All that water and not one person has a line in."

You know how you can't get a song out of your mind? For the next three days I went around singing "Eatin' what you want and doin' what you choose." For a long time I had wondered what kind of people we'd be away from the daily routine of sorting socks and filling up ice cube trays. We had taken vacations, but they always ended up somewhere between a church camp and elective surgery. What would it be like to live in elegance for a couple of weeks? To sweep into a dining room in a long gown or strike up a conversation at a ship's railing with a mysterious stranger wearing an ascot?

I had seen enough episodes of "The Love Boat" to know that no one came off a cruise ship the same person as when he boarded one. I looked upon it as a Club Bed, so to speak, with everyone dressing up each evening like he was going to the prom, throwing confetti at one another, and drinking champagne out of glasses that didn't smell like creme rinse.

"How do you feel about an adventure on water?" I whispered softly to my husband one night.

"Did your contacts fall down the commode again?"

"I'm talking about a cruise. We need a cruise."

"Why?"

"Because we are in a rut. We need some romance in our lives."

"And a cruise is going to make the difference," he said flatly.

"Evelyn Grimshaw told me that lovemaking burns a hundred and twenty-five calories. She and Dan came home from the Caribbean and both looked absolutely anorexic."

"If you believe that," he said, "you believe that Gilligan set out on a three-hour trip from Hawaii with enough luggage to last Lovey and Thurston Howell III and Ginger for seven seasons."

"With cork luggage? It could happen," I said stubbornly.

After a couple of months of serious whining, I finally convinced him that a cruise would be a relaxing vacation for both of us. There would be no packing and unpacking clothes, no on and off buses, no road maps or rental cars, delayed airline flights or pesky tipping. For one-price-pays-all, we could just relax and rediscover one another.

We booked passage on a Norwegian ship leaving Copenhagen. For two weeks we would cruise through the fjords of Norway before returning to port. On the second two-week leg, we'd visit Sweden, Finland, Germany, and Russia, for a total of one month.

From the moment we stepped across the gangplank at Copenhagen, I experienced a feeling I had not had before . . . acute insecurity. I really couldn't explain it. As I looked around at the elegance and the efficiency, I knew that my husband and I were the only two people left on the planet who had never been on a cruise ship before. Everyone was richer, thinner, and smarter than us.

I knew in my heart they carried passports dog-eared from use, had new underwear and old money. Face it, we were the only couple aboard who paid for the trip with a credit union check and carried borrowed luggage full of borrowed clothes that carried a warning, "Sweat in it and you clean it." Not a word was spoken, but everyone I talked to had signed up for the nine P.M. dinner seating. I knew we would be the only two peasants eating alone at seven in that huge dining room.

Romance was going to be a challenge. Especially when you're married to a man who lists dressing up every night right up there with a root canal. Not to mention the downside of washing out his only ruffled evening shirt every night in the basin and hanging it in the shower to dry.

Then there was the motion problem. When I threw up in a standing ashtray filled with sand just outside the dining room before we left the dock, I knew we would never whisper anything in one another's ear except, "Get me a cold towel."

The ship was commanded by Captain Gunther, whose English was limited. All he ever said to me was, "I am Norwegian. There is no immediate danger." He always smiled when he said it.

I have to admit the first couple of days aboard

the floating cookie were special. The fjords were stunning, the Norwegian people were a delight, and I was beginning to get over my low self-esteem. Also, we could still zip up our clothes. Life doesn't get any better than that.

However, by the time we made port at Tromsø, the capital of the Arctic, I bought maternity underwear. My clothes were getting a little snug and the cabin seemed to be closing in on us. Every time we turned around we kept bumping into each other. Actually, we were closing in on it.

One day at lunch, I said to my husband, "Why are you wearing a life preserver?" He said, "I'm not. That's me."

As the lazy days wore on, there was a rush at the gift shop for the racks of Diane Freis dresses. (This is a designer who specializes in dresses that are wildly colorful, never wrinkle, are one-size-fits-all, and have elastic waistbands.) On the day we docked at Bergen to watch a group of Norwegian folk dancers, more than a dozen of us wore them ashore. We looked like the next act.

Late one night as the alarm by the bed went off, my husband turned sleepily and asked, "Is it morning already?"

"Get up," I ordered. "It's time for the midnight buffet on the promenade deck. They're serving Scarlet Ox Tongue in Jelly and Vendolhoo Indian Lamb Curry."

He swung his feet to the side of his bed and

rubbed his eyes. "Again!" he snapped. "Why can't they just serve plain old Roast Cornish Hen Montmorency or Cretan Potatoes?" As he pulled on his sweats, he continued, "This has got to stop."

"What has got to stop?"

"How many meals are we eating a day?"

"Seventeen . . . eighteen, tops," I said defensively. "Is that a problem?"

"If we keep this up, we'll have our own zip code."

"At the early bird, all we have is a roll and coffee."

"Followed by an eight-course breakfast," he added.

"No one forces you to have a bouillon break just before lunch."

"Who had a gun at your head for the tea with the sandwiches and cookies?" he countered.

"It wasn't me who pigged out at the happy hour with all those hot canapés and hors d'oeuvres."

"And I didn't see it ruining your dinner . . . or the pizza party or the predawn breakfast afterward."

"Look," I said, "if you think I'm gaining weight, just say so."

"Let me put it this way. If someone wants to show home movies, all you have to do is wear white slacks and bend over."

He slammed out of the stateroom.

I looked in the mirror. He was right. I was beginning to dress like the Statue of Liberty. I held out my arms and fanned the skin that hung like a stage curtain. It was only a matter of time before fourteen tourists would fit in my arm. I couldn't go home like this.

When I joined him at the buffet, I had a plan. From here on in, we would take advantage of all the activities aboard the ship and maybe work off some of the food. He agreed.

If there's anything a cruise ship does and does well, it keeps you busy. And they certainly have the staff for it. When I went to Fitness on the Fantail with Jennifer, my husband went to the library with Carole for the ship's daily quiz. When I learned how to make rosettes out of radishes with Chef Andre, my husband was in a shuffleboard tournament with Bruce. I danced the tango with Fern and Phillipe. He practiced golf swings with Phil.

I wanted him to tour the bridge one afternoon with Captain Gunther, but he was busy playing bingo with Hal and Barbara.

We were like two ships passing one another in the dark. When he was at table tennis with Sibyl and the gang, I was doing calligraphy with Lotus Flower. He went off trapshooting with Hank while I played bridge.

One night when I joined Debbie Sunshine at

the piano in the Mediterranean Lounge, I met my husband by chance. "I miss you," I said.

"Me too," he responded.

"I won at bingo today," I said.

"You want to go to the casino?"

"I'd love to," I said, "but I have a rehearsal. The passengers are doing *The Sound of Music*. I'm one of the nuns."

"Perfect casting," he snapped and walked away.

We rarely saw each other, but one night as I whipped into the stateroom from my needlepoint class, my husband was stretched out on the bed. I asked him what he was doing in the room.

"I'm exhausted," he said. "Do you suppose that for one night I wouldn't have to put on a tuxedo and tie and go to the dining room and eat shrimp out of a carved ice swan and dance until one A.M.?"

I sat on the bed beside him. "Tonight you can forget the tux," I said softly. "This is the evening of the ship's costume party, remember? Everyone is supposed to appear in a costume made from stuff you have on hand."

"You're kidding," he said.

"Not to worry. I have a costume for you. You are going to wear my green tights and green aerobics leotard and go as a zucchini."

By the time we returned to Copenhagen, we were barely speaking to each other. Familiarity did not breed children as Mark Twain once remarked. It bred irritability and sniping. We were sluggish from carrying around extra pounds and exhausted from all that leisure.

The last night at sea before we docked, we both sat stiffly at the captain's table and sipped the complimentary wine provided with our dinner.

I looked around the table. All of us had talked one another to death. We had eaten at least one hundred and ninety-six meals with these people. We had heard all their stories, relived their travels, laughed at their jokes, and perused their brag albums of grandchildren. We had spent more time with them on buses and land tours than we had with our families. The cruise crowd didn't have the same staple manifest as the guided tour, but there were stereotypes.

There was Edith Purge, the dessert queen. She was traveling alone, and because she ate everything that didn't attack her first, she wore caftans to bed. Her philosophy was, "You're paying through the nose for all of this, honey, so you might just as well eat it." When the maitre d' asked if she wanted the seven or the nine o'clock dinner seating, she answered, "Yes." She took three rolls of film one day—all of the dessert table.

There were the Tweeds, a no-nonsense couple from Maine. They were both into fitness and felt their mission in life was to ruin your appreciation of food. I can't enjoy a hot dog today without thinking of their pig-lips lecture. Every morning at six the Tweeds hit the decks, and heaven help anyone who interfered with their brisk, goose-stepping walk.

The Borings, Winston and Charlotte, appeared every evening like they were shot full of Novocain. The only time they spoke was to drop another name of a country they had traveled. They had been to all the African nations before the name changes and were the only couple at the table who knew how to wield a fish knife. That appeared to be their only talent.

The Craigs were an interesting couple. He drank and she changed clothes eight or ten times a day. One night I noted a seasickness patch behind her ear. I swear it had a G for Gucci on it. We get a Christmas card from them every year. Our name is misspelled.

At the farewell dinner, Captain Gunther summoned our wine steward, who brought a bottle of aquavit to the table. The steward explained it was a strong Norwegian drink. You slug down a shot of it and chase it with a sip of beer. Two of them, he said, and you would forget who you came with. The captain had slugged down the first round when I leaned over and said, "I read where you weren't supposed to mix wine with aquavit."

The captain looked at me blankly, then broke

into a smile. "I am Norwegian. There is no immediate danger."

My father always said, "There's no such thing as a free lunch." I figured what did he know. My father never went on a cruise ship where he ate fifteen meals a day without so much as dropping a single dime under the plate. He never had people fluffing up his pillow, taking an empty glass out of his hand, putting up a deck chair for him without a palm extended. Everything was included in the package.

On the last day aboard the cruise ship, I realized my father was right. There is a moment when you have to pay the piper for letting you dance around the decks without a checkbook.

Just before you make port, you are encouraged to show your appreciation to all those people who befriended you.

You leave a tip for the deck chair steward who raced to open your chair every morning, for the towel steward who stood around like a midwife waiting to wipe beads of perspiration from your forehead, and for the cocktail steward who brought you liquids stuck to a little napkin.

You put a little something in an envelope for the maitre d' who showed you to your table each evening, to the wine steward who helped you select "something fruity but not pretentious," and to your waiter who remembered your name from day one . . . such a nice boy.

You tip the bread server and the busboy, the luggage handler and the bartender, your favorite cocktail waitress and the girl singer with the band who led the group singing "Happy Birthday."

You tip the young girl who turned down your bed and the one who made it and cleaned the room each day. You tip the beautician who did your hair and the room steward who served you dinner in your room several nights and the croupier in the casino.

As my husband returned his flat wallet to his pocket, he said, "I hope we have enough left for cab fare home."

"Look at it this way," I said. "It took two inches off your hips."

Shopping

Everyone has role models.

Mine is a dream team of shoppers who have become known as the Four Horsemen of the National Shopping League (NSL):

Imelda Marcos, formerly of the Philippines
Nancy Reagan, United States
Michèle Duvalier, Haiti
Jacqueline Onassis, United States

I tell you there is nothing that gets my heart beating faster than to watch a team of shoppers who are physically fit, mentally alert, and professionally trained put their talents to work in the store aisles.

We're not talking amateurs here who play in the Discount Bowls and fumble around fifteen minutes to read price tags. No siree, we're talking world-class competitors who spend $10,430 on bed sheets in one day and who buy two hundred twenty place settings of dishes at $952 a crack. They're the stuff of which musicals are made, where you come out of the theater humming, "Don't Cry for Me Valentino."

It's hard to break into the major shopping league. I remember how Raisa Gorbachev caused a flap when she dropped a few bucks on jewelry during a trip to London a few years ago. Critics in the Soviet Union had a cow claiming she was caught up in the decadence of western ways.

The truth is Russian shoppers are a good two hundred years behind the rest of the world. While they were sitting over there stockpiling missiles and connecting dots all over those floral print dresses, the rest of the world was turning its technology toward malls and major shopping emporiums.

London launched Harrods, Japan positioned Issey Miyake, Hong Kong perfected a fabulous silk factory called Kaiser Estates Phase I, and frankly, if I saw Bergdorf-Goodman catalogs aimed toward my country from the United States, I'd panic.

Have you ever seen a Russian woman make the National Shopping League? No, and you won't. I knew Raisa was an amateur when she never thought to ask herself, "Why isn't Nancy Reagan going to Reykjavík?" The answer should have been obvious. Why would anyone go to a barren countryside that had never heard of Adolfo?

My husband says he thinks I'm ready for the NSL, but he just says that to make me feel good. The only time I am challenged is when I go on vacation. I live by a couple of standard rules.

1. Never buy anything that fits under an airline seat.
2. Buy in haste. Repent in leisure. Face it, you'll never get this way again.
3. Most people back home will believe anything is tasteful just so long as it comes from a foreign country. It doesn't hurt to leave foreign price tags on. (12 million lire sounds impressive. They don't know the exchange is $3.39 in U.S. dollars.)
4. Never buy clothes in a country where the women wear overcoats and cover their heads with babushkas.
5. Never ask, "Do I need this?" The answer is always no.

Shopping for souvenirs is one of the few joys of traveling for me. I will buy anything. Nothing is too tacky for me to lug home. I have purchased key chains made out of boar's hair, tasteless T-shirts that read I WENT TO NEW GUINEA AND NO ONE ATE

ME, paperweights with the Loch Ness monster in them, and, from Mexico, a band of dipped-in-wax frogs with unbelievable fear on their faces, playing musical instruments.

I have purchased coconuts with Indian faces, inflated blowfish, rugs with camel dung on them, little outhouses with doors that fly open and reveal a mountaineer sitting on a one-holer reading a newspaper.

Also, Eskimos with candle wicks coming out of their heads, tape measures in metric, and pillow tops with the Kennedy brothers that glow in the dark.

I have seen travelers anguish over a $2 hermetically sealed four-leaf clover like they're buying a condo in Florida. I look at it this way. This is a one-shot opportunity, and if one day I can run across a bottle opener with a picture of Mount Vesuvius on it in the stove drawer, and it sparks a memory, it's worth it.

In Istanbul, there is a giant spice market lined with tubs of spices all bearing their identification—in Turkish. I bought two pounds of a mound of green stuff, thinking it was mint. It was henna.

Shopping is basically a game of wits. Especially in Turkey, where every male citizen over the age of twelve is a carpet salesman. They are like a film of dust that settles over the country. In fact, there are so many of them that when tourists see them coming, their only defense is to hold a crucifix in front of them like they are being confronted by Barnabas Collins and yell, "Back! Back!" That is why they have some of the most creative approaches I have ever seen.

The "911 to the rescue" approach

As you are standing on a street corner surrounded by six carpet salesmen, a man will wave them all away in Turkish and turn to you and say in perfect English, "Aren't they pests? I'm from America too. What state are you from?" It doesn't matter what state you give. He has been there.

He will tell you he and his wife came to Turkey a couple of years ago to live and will offer to buy you a cup of coffee in friendship. The coffee will be served in a (get outta here) carpet shop a few blocks from where you are standing. He will tell you he is buying carpets for a large firm in New York. If there's anything you like he can get you a good price. They ship.

The "trust me, I'm not selling carpets" approach

You are snapping a picture in the park when a young man says, "That is a great camera. How much you pay for it?" You shrug and give him some figure and he opens up his billfold and says,

"I'd like to buy it." You smile (big mistake) and say, "No, thank you." He follows you around for the next two days talking about it until you finally say, "I really don't want to sell my camera. Goodbye." Then he says, "Would you like to look at my carpets? They're better and cheaper than anyone else's." They take American Express.

The "blind date" approach

This is a popular one. The salesman will walk close to you and say, *"Parlez vous Français?"* You shake your head. *"Sprechen Sie Deutsch?"* You answer no. After he hits every country in Rand McNally, he makes a stab at English. Once you have a language in common, he will stick to you like pantyhose in Phoenix in July . . . telling you how great his carpets are. He offers to lie on the customs declaration.

The "thirst for knowledge" approach

By the side of the road will be a large Bedouin tent. At the gate you will be met by a young man who speaks English and is anxious to explain the customs of the nomad tribes and the way they lived. It is no coincidence that the floor is solid with wall-to-wall Turkish carpets. From there, he will proceed to where the artisans are dyeing wool using natural fibers. Next to them are women in front of looms who are tying knots faster than he can say "Come, look at the finished product in our showroom."

I bought a carpet. He said I had exquisite taste.

At one time I amassed so much junk that when I went through customs the officer asked, "How long have you been gone?"

"Three weeks," I said.

"It's impossible to buy all this stuff in three weeks. Did you see any of the country?"

"What country?" I asked.

He waved me on.

There are few certainties when you travel. One of them is that the moment you arrive in a foreign country, the American dollar will fall like a stone.

We have never traveled anywhere where the American dollar was strong . . . with the exception of Mexico. Maybe it was firm when we left New York, but by the time we got to our destination, $20 wouldn't buy us a newspaper.

We have paid $10 for a soft drink in Sweden and $12 for a hamburger in Russia. For two bowls of soup and two soft drinks in Japan, we forked over $42.

My husband reacts to all of this with the grimness of Louis Rukeyser. I, on the other hand, am struck with an unreal approach to it. Foreign currency seems like Monopoly play money to me. I think nothing of dropping a suitcase full of Italian lire for a cup of coffee.

Every country we have visited acts like its dollar is king . . . until you go to turn it back in. Then the country doesn't want it. No one wants its own money back with the exception of Russia, who doesn't want it back so much as it doesn't want the rubles out of its sight for fear someone will find out how much they are really worth.

My husband is never without one of those little currency decoders. You just punch into it the current rate of exchange, push a few buttons, and it lights up the answer.

I have my own system. I just drop the last three zeros, divide by two, add my age (not the real one, but the one that appears on my bio), and drop a decimal point third from the right. It's close enough.

When that fails, you just grab all the money you own in your hands, hold it out, and let them take what they want.

One should never let the fate of the U.S. dollar get in the way of shopping. I don't understand people who can go abroad and come back with nothing to declare but diarrhea. Bartering is an art form. In San Miguel de Allende in Mexico, I saw a six-foot wooden statue of Don Quixote that I figured would look great in our courtyard.

"Cuanto?" I asked

The salesman wrote down $150.

I laughed and headed toward the door. He called me back and wrote down $100. I began to hum and pick lint off my dress. He kept writing until he got to $77.

"Sold," I said.

I paid a man down the street from the shop $42 to crate it. I paid $120 to have it put on a train for Laredo, Texas, and another $320 to have a truck bring it to my doorstep. When people ask me how much I paid for it, I only give the base price.

Shopping is probably the most underrated contact sport in the world. It's especially challenging when you're in countries where the stores close for siestas, like Spain, Mexico, or Greece. Most of these stores are open only from ten until one. They reopen again from three to five-thirty. You must shop quickly. I survive in this frantic atmosphere only because I have no taste.

When shoppers fantasize, the streets of Hong Kong is the place that comes to mind. The city is one giant mall. We spent four days there dragging through miles of stalls and acres of shops. I didn't take time to eat or sleep. At one time there was serious talk of a catheter as biological functions were slowing me down. When I returned home I had credit card burns on the palms of both hands. Shopping in Hong Kong, purported to be the Shopping Olympics, was fun, but where was the challenge? Inquiring "Did you buy anything in Hong Kong?" is like asking "Does the Pope work Sundays?"

At some point in my travels, I knew my shopping skills would be tested. I felt I was ready.

South America

After flying twenty-three hundred miles across the Pacific from Chile, it was a relief to see the small outline of Rapa Nui—Easter Island—beneath us.

I had so looked forward to the trip to South America. Everything I had read about it had only heightened my enthusiasm: those heavenly wool ponchos in the marketplace that you could pick up for $6 . . . stunning silver necklaces and earrings for a song . . . not to mention the exquisite hand-embroidered blouses and sweaters that I could give as Christmas gifts.

As we claimed our luggage on the tarmac, a chill went through my body. I shrugged it off. I would feel better when we got into town . . . in the center of things. But the feeling didn't go away. As we rode by small clusters of houses and an occasional grocery store, I whispered to my husband, "There's something strange about this place."

"I know." He smiled. "I feel it too. No lush forests, no tropical birds, no white beaches or dramatic waterfalls, no buildings of any stature, only the hollow winds that whistle over this barren countryside and those giant, mysterious stone men with vacant eyes rising majestically out of the ground."

"Why are you talking like Jacques Cousteau? Look around you! Do you realize we have not seen one single gift shop in this place? I am supposed to spend four days on an island that has no gift shops?"

"How can you possibly be bored surrounded by all of this symbolism and mystery?"

"Look at me," I commanded. "Do you know what you're dealing with? You are looking at a shallow woman who left while the Pope was saying Mass at St. Peter's in Rome to buy a splinter from the cross on which Christ purportedly died, from a man in the square wearing fifteen watches on his forearm."

"Knowing you," he said, "you'll rise to the challenge."

I joined our tour group and rode around in the little buses. I had no choice. We poked around caves, volcanoes, and excavation sites where they were restoring these monoliths, and I had to admit I was intrigued by it all. Some of the statues had been toppled and rested facedown in the open areas. Some were still in caves where work on them had been abandoned. Sometimes there would be groupings of them. A few had cinder hats, others had larger ears. But they all had several things in common. They were huge, had no eyes, and were a mystery to anthropologists who for years had come to Easter Island in an attempt to piece together a culture that had left few clues.

"You see," said my husband, "I knew you'd be fascinated by this place. I'll bet you've even forgotten about shopping."

"I love this place," I said, "but if I don't find something to buy within the next twenty-four hours, I am going to become physically ill."

Down from our hotel (which had no gift shop) was a large platform on which seven of these statues—about sixty feet tall—faced away from the sea. They looked like giant targets on the gun range of a police academy. Since South Americans dine after ten o'clock at night, it created a problem for me. I am asleep by nine-thirty at night. So each evening at dusk I took a candy bar and bag of potato chips and joined the Stone Seven.

As I dangled my feet from the stone pedestal, I looked up at them, studied their expressionless faces, and figured they alone held the secret of why Easter Island had no gift shops. It probably had something to do with a woman who gave them bad shells.

The next morning, I hung around the hotel and asked one of the Easter Islanders where you could buy souvenirs.

He reported there were many statues and much jewelry made by the natives, but they would rather not exchange their wares for money. He had my attention.

It seems Easter Island holds the distinction of being the most remote spot on the face of the earth. Its closest neighbor is Pitcairn Island, twelve hundred miles to the west. Therefore, it is often cut off from basic supplies needed to exist. Tourists fly in regularly from Chile, but the cost of sending supplies by air is prohibitive. A ship is scheduled to come twice a year, but they are at the whim of rough seas, and supplies must often be transferred to smaller boats. The carvings could be had for a box of aspirin, a pair of scissors, shampoo, or shoes.

I could handle that. I just had to know the rules. That afternoon, I visited a man carving statues and dropped to my knees as if I had just found the only crap game in town.

Before we departed Easter Island, I had a suitcase of beautiful wood carvings of the statues, some wonderful jewelry, and several watercolors.

My husband left without his running shoes, shaving cream, Swiss army knife, a pair of jeans, a cotton pullover, and his warm-ups.

If his astigmatism had been right, I could have traded his prescription sunglasses for a beach towel with a monolith stamped on it.

He asked, "Why didn't you trade your own clothes?" That was the weird part. They're cut off from the rest of the world . . . but they still have taste.

If I thought Easter Island was a shopper's challenge, I was about to face the second biggest test of my buying career. Our next stop was the Galapagos, off the coast of Ecuador.

The plane landed on a bare strip with nothing but a lean-to nearby to protect arriving passengers from the sun. From there, we were herded onto a small boat to cruise the archipelago that had played a major role in our understanding of the process of evolution.

When I heard that most of the islands were void of people, my heart sank. Any day now my husband would get a sympathy card from American Express on the death of his wife. I had not charged anything in two weeks.

I wouldn't have minded sloshing ashore with the sea lion swimming around me if there had been a Stuckey's on the beach. Even sliding down a mountain of volcanic ash would have been bearable if I knew at the bottom there would be a little boutique with note cards and scented soaps. But there was nothing.

I was being held captive on a no-frills ship of geologists, zoologists, and botanists who cared about the preservation of the world but nothing about toilet tissue. I hate to make generalizations, but there is a definite correlation between smart people and little regard for creature comforts.

The little ship bobbed along for days from island to island studying the blue-footed booby and marine iguanas. We had our pictures taken astride a giant tortoise. We crawled over sharp, jagged rocks, splashed through water, and hid out in tall grass to watch frigate birds display themselves. (I felt dirty doing that.)

On one island, scientists were overseeing the reproduction of turtles. There were literally thousands of baby turtles crawling around in a large pit. As I turned to my husband, my eyes brightened and I opened my mouth to speak.

"Forget it!" he said. "They are not going to paint Galapagos on their backs and sell them."

At nights, I joined the group in the ship's small lounge to listen to lectures, watch slides, and make notes on what we were to see the next day. No one suspected that in college in response to the question, "What is a chinook?" I wrote in, "The name of the guy I just broke up with."

This was not a crowd that was interested in souvenirs. They were purists who came on this vacation to learn something about our planet. If they had known where I was coming from, they would have studied me.

After five days in the Galapagos, I took my credit cards out of my bra and returned them to my billfold. I had suffered my first defeat.

There are few places in the world where you really have to fight to leave your money. You show me a religious shrine and I'll show you a T-shirt that reads I GOT A PEEK AT THE POPE or LIVING IT UP AT LOURDES.

One place I was prepared to go home empty-handed was the North Cape. It is a barren district on the Arctic Sea made accessible only by a road that winds through an area that can best be described as desolate. There are a few small lakes, sparse vegetation, and herds of reindeer brought to forage during the summer.

We traveled by bus for about an hour out of Honningsvag, Norway, before we reached the tents of a village of Laplanders. They were as curious about us as we were about them. As the souvenir queen, I quickly admitted defeat.

Our driver started the motor of the bus as a warning to a passenger who had not yet boarded. It was my husband. Finally, he emerged from the tent of a Laplander holding a long roll under his arm. The moment he entered the bus, we knew what it was . . . a reindeer skin. Despite the bitter cold, people gasped as they threw open their windows and covered their faces from the smell. In the name of compassion, we sat in the back of the bus.

Back on the ship the reindeer skin continued to smell. I sprayed it with deodorant and perfume. We rolled it in paper and stored it under the bed. We stuffed it in the closet and zipped it in the luggage. It didn't work. The odor permeated our hair and our wardrobe. Whenever we entered the dining room, someone would sniff and say, "Don't be surprised if a herd of male reindeer swim out to the ship and ask you to dance."

When we arrived home, my husband said, "Where are we going to put this?"

"You mean after it dies?"

"C'mon," he said, "I hardly notice it anymore."

He put it in the garage over his workbench.

We haven't parked the car in the garage since.

Flying for Peanuts

In my mind, I always imagined the little Wright Brothers sitting on a curb in Dayton, Ohio, talking about their future.

Wilbur says, "You know, Orville, it's getting crowded down here. We ought to invent something that gets people off the ground and into the air so they can fly from one place to another with wings."

"How do we do that, Wilbur?"

"First, we have to get something we can stuff people into . . . like a CAT scanner."

"CAT scanners haven't been invented yet, Wilbur. Besides, it sounds claustrophobic."

"OK then, something like a silo. We'd put in a couple of windows."

"What would you do about breathing?" asks Orville.

"We'd pressurize the cabin," says his brother. "Of course, if something malfunctioned, we'd have little bags of oxygen that would drop automatically in front of their faces. People love gimmicks."

"I don't know," muses Orville. "What if passengers got sick?"

"No problem-o," says Wilbur. "For a couple of bucks, we could put little paper barf bags in the seat pocket with instructions on how to throw up in two languages. This would be a first-class operation."

"Could you land these silos in the cities?" asks Orville.

"Are you crazy? We'd set the passengers down in a cornfield miles from town and let them get in any way they could. In fact, I visualize putting the Cincinnati airport in Kentucky."

"What about food?"

"We'd give 'em food they can't identify. That way they won't know if it's good or bad."

"You're a genius, Wilbur."

"I see it as a country club of the clouds," offers his brother. "A place where you can unwind and not have a care in the world. People will get their flight insurance in the lobby, go through security and have all their belongings X-rayed for guns and knives before they board the plane. After the attendants have given them the evacuation procedures in the event of loss of air pressure and demonstrated how to use the life jackets in the event they ditch over water, they're free to relax."

"Sounds great, Wilbur. How much do you suppose we would have to pay each person to fly it?"

"Orville, Orville, you just don't get it, do you? We don't pay them to fly. They pay us."

At this point, I picture Orville backing slowly away from his brother until he is out of range, and then he runs breathlessly to his father and shouts, "Daddy! Come quick! Wilbur's bicycle just slipped its chain."

Most of us have had a love/hate relationship with airlines. We love them when they're on time; we hate them the rest of the time. But the fact that we climb on and off of them by the millions in a cavalier fashion proves that we have not lost our adventurous spirit. We are somehow willing to forgive them for just about anything.

A passenger was sucked through a plane window on a flight from Portland to Seattle. "It was an incredibly strong force," he was quoted as saying. "I tried twice to get back."

Passengers finally succeeded in getting him back through the twelve-by-eighteen-inch window. After he was treated in Seattle for his injuries, he climbed back on the same plane for the return trip to Portland.

I have been on a plane where the doors were secured, announcements had been made, and we all settled back to leave the gate when there was a knock on the door and the pilot and co-pilot were standing outside trying to board.

In another incident, the plane could not take off because we were hopelessly stuck to the jetport and an hour later, it looked like we would have to be surgically removed from one another.

There have been moments when flying is sometimes like pledge week on PBS. I wasn't aboard this particular flight, but on a London run to the Madeira Islands, the pilot's voice came over the intercom, "Ladies and gentlemen, we have a flight problem. Would you please contribute as much cash as possible so we can buy fuel to continue our journey?"

The passengers passed the hat and came up with $2,000, enough to buy 14,300 pounds of fuel to reach London. It seems the Porto Santo airport in Madeira refused to recognize the pilot's airline credit card and demanded cash.

There are no two people on an airplane who have paid the same price for a seat. Think about it and it will make you crazy. Some are relatives of airline employees who pay nothing, some are traveling on amassed mileage coupons, and some are on super savers where they travel on Tuesday morning only during the months when oysters are in season if they buy their tickets at high tide on the day they were born.

But one class distinction has remained: first class. These are all people who are either on expense accounts or are taking a pet to the "David Letterman Show." They are divided from the peasants by a limp blue curtain.

I always wondered how long it would be before the little people in tourist, economy, and super saver seats stormed the Limp Curtain to protest inequality.

How long would they sit there and watch that little curtain being snapped together leaving them suspicious and classless? It's the stuff of which revolutions are made.

Well, it happened. A California woman in the coach section was awarded $8,000 a while back in a suit that alleged that a first-class passenger cursed and shoved her as she stood in line to use the bathroom in first-class. (On a scale of guts, that's equivalent to landing a plane in Red Square in the Soviet Union.)

The victim admitted she pushed through the Limp Curtain as a last resort. She could not reach "her own" facilities because a drink cart blocked the aisle. The defendant charged that the woman "trespassed in first class and violated his priority right to use the bathroom."

Good heavens, do you know what this means? Next thing you know, a super saver passenger will try to infiltrate his garment bag into a first class compartment or try to inhale first class smoke on an international flight. It won't stop there.

First-class travel has always been a mystique shrouded in fantasy to most Americans. They visualize it as a place on the plane where skirts and flight times are shorter, entertainment is live, and bathrooms are big enough to shut the door without standing on the seat.

Some people imagine women with tiaras, large bosoms, and lace fans throwing back their heads and laughing, "Let 'em eat stale sheet cake and green noodles back there."

The irony is that the Limp Curtain dividing first class from tourist was never meant to keep the tourists in the dark—but the first-class passengers. No one wants them to know that their cocktail service is longer so attendants can get tourist class served first. They want to keep secret the fact that although they are paying twice the fare, the food is the same and they have half as many bathrooms.

Recently, I was riding in business class when I saw a first-class passenger spying at us through the Limp Curtain. He knows too much for them to let him live.

The airlines try. They have rules to cover everything. Ironically, the things that airlines concern themselves with are the things that never really happen.

How many headlines do you see: GLASS NOT COLLECTED BY ATTENDANT BEFORE TAKEOFF RESPONSIBLE FOR FIRST-CLASS DROWNING? Or, LUGGAGE NOT PUSHED ALL THE WAY UNDER SEAT CAUSES PLANE TO PLUMMET?

Here they are worried sick about keeping the door of the cockpit locked to protect them from hijackers and a captain of a British Airways flight is sucked out of his seat through the windshield.

I'm not minimizing security. It is a major concern of airlines and we should all take it as seriously as they do. However, when I see a terrorist in custody splattered over the front pages of my newspaper, it is always a mystery to me how he got by in the first place. He is usually an evil-looking man (or woman) with crazy eyes. He has no luggage and clutches with both hands a gym bag that holds an Uzi automatic. Yet, he breezed right through all that technical equipment. What did they think the Uzi was? A giant curling iron?

Then I am reminded of a small airport in Iowa where I watched a little old man in his eighties with no teeth, a voice like Gomer Pyle's, suspenders and belt on his trousers, plaid shirt, and a billed cap with Ralston Purina stamped on it. He didn't seem to fit your basic terrorist profile. But when he stepped through the security passage, a buzzer went off. He emptied his change on a tray and went through again. It buzzed. They claimed his car keys and his suspenders, which had metal on them. Five times he went through, stripping as he went. It was finally ascertained he was trying to smuggle aboard a half stick of gum covered with foil.

We've all been relieved of "weapons." I've had needlepoint scissors that couldn't cut hot butter taken from me for "safekeeping." One man said they took his cigarette lighter because there was a potentially explosive mix of chemicals. "My wife's cosmetics case probably had more potential for exploding," he said. But the most ludicrous example I can think of was my teenage son who was bringing back a Masai spear as a souvenir from Africa.

Two security officers boarded the plane, escorted him off, and stood by while he checked the spear through with his luggage. I had to wonder when was the last time Great Britain was attacked by spear.

The idea of not blocking the aisle with things that do not fit under your seat is a joke. Can you imagine what a smooth exit you'd make when the person in front of you reclines his seat, embedding your snack table tray in your stomach?

I would be remiss if I didn't point out the greatest hazard of flying: the food.

There are some mysteries of airline food that need to be addressed:

More than six drinks of Snappy Tom will simulate a heart attack.

Hermetically sealed peanuts are really time
   capsules and never meant to be opened in
   this century.
Never eat anything that blinks first.
Airline steaks are done when they say they
   are done.
No matter what you order, the entrée you
   didn't order will look better.
Some of the best fiction writers got their
   start writing airline menus.
The longer the cocktail hour, the more
   pathetic the entrées.
When you see pilots eating ice cream before
   they board, that is a clue they are ruining
   their dinner before it ruins them.

I certainly don't wish to imply that airlines are
not sensitive to your problems. When passengers
complained a few years ago that airline schedules
were a disgrace and late arrivals were the norm
and not the exception, they quickly did something about it.

They added thirty minutes to all their arrival
times.

I could have done that.

A flight that normally takes fifty minutes now
shows eighty minutes on the schedule, so that
when it arrives "on time" you're not sure if it is
the "real" time it takes to fly that distance or the
padded time that is logged for the FAA.

In defense of airlines, there are a lot of reasons for being late:

A passenger refused to sit down and they
   were thirty seconds late leaving the jetport.
They left late because they were waiting for
   late-arriving baggage to be boarded. (Stand
   back. Noses grow on this one.)
"Someone left a cargo door open" gives you
   a warm glow, as does, "We seem to be
   missing a crew."

The rules of aviation are still being written. Recently, a couple were escorted from a plane because they smelled bad. (Then again, it could have been the entrée.) In another incident, police and a pair of handcuffs awaited a passenger who saw fit to "steal the music" aboard a plane by using his own headphones. I don't even want to imagine what would happen if they found someone reading lips watching a movie he didn't pay for.

An observation is sometimes made that Wilbur and Orville Wright would be amazed at the crowded skies that resulted from their invention eighty-eight years ago. Maybe not.

Somehow I can see Wilbur sitting up there some-where in the clouds smiling when passengers are reassured before takeoff that their cushions will flotate if they have to. He is gleeful when we all sit there like flies on a doughnut while flight attendants ask us to cover our faces while they come through with an aerosol spray for bugs before we land in the Bahamas.

When we line up obediently for surveillance while a dog sniffs our pillboxes containing estrogen, I have a feeling Orville is there too . . . shaking his head and saying, "I can't believe they bought it."

Language

In September 1987, I was asked to introduce His Holiness Pope John Paul II, who was to preside over a papal Mass in Sun Devil Stadium, Tempe, Arizona.

I was humbled by the honor and wanted desperately to do something special. I decided to welcome him in Polish, his native tongue.

The only Pole I knew was a seamstress who did alterations for me from time to time, so I said to her, "Tell me how to welcome the Pope in his own language."

On the night before his arrival, I rehearsed the speech before a couple of priests in charge of the event. I took a deep breath before my big finish, "*Arizona vita oitsa sven-tego yana pavwa druu-uuugeggo.*"

One of the priests said to me, "Why would you want to tell the Pope his luggage is lost?"

I am not good with language.

Spain

Sometimes I dazzled myself with my efficiency. I had the signed contracts for the rented Spanish villa in my handbag. I had triumphed over the logistics of getting eight members of our family to rendezvous at the Barcelona airport. The reserved rental cars were waiting to take us to the small town of Palafrugell, where we would be met by a staff that included a gardener, a housekeeper, and a cook. Every detail was in place for the perfect holiday on the "wild coast" of Spain.

We had never planned a vacation quite like it before.

At the villa as I alighted from the car, the staff came forward like a scene straight out of an

English novel. The older woman smiled broadly before she extended her hand in welcome. "*Buenos dias, senora.*"

"Hi," I said warmly in return, pumping her hand.

"*Espero que tinguis un bon viadge?*"

"Right. So, where do you want our luggage?"

"*Si teniu alguna pregunda som aqui per a servir-vos.*"

"You do speak English, don't you?"

"*Voldrieu una copa de vi i una mica de formadge?*"

My husband whispered, "They don't speak English."

"Of course they speak English," I said. At this point I used my usual speaking voice when conversing with foreigners. I place myself squarely in front of their faces, raise my voice and shout slowly, "DO—YOU—SPEAK—ENGLISH?"

"They're not hard of hearing," said my husband. "They're only Spanish."

By this time, the staff were beginning to talk among themselves. I once again intervened. "*Hablas Ingles, por favor?*"

All three shook their heads vehemently. "*No no, senora. Habla Catalan.*"

"What's Catalan?" I asked my husband.

"It's a language spoken in Northern Spain. It's Spanish with a twist."

"They don't speak English," I announced to the group.

"What about those nine credit hours of Spanish you took in college?"

"The only thing I remember is the Lord's Prayer."

"It's worth a shot," said my dad.

I couldn't believe that I had overlooked something this important. In most large cities, English is spoken . . . somewhere. But here in this small community, it was nonexistent.

My husband drew me aside. "Let me get this straight. We are spending the next three weeks in a house where the only way we can communicate with the staff is by prayer?"

"I remember a few words here and there," I lied. "Besides, there are bound to be a few phrases in the back of the guidebook."

I must say at this point that it boggles the mind to read what expressions writers of these books consider important for travelers. The phrases included: "May I have a kilo of oranges?" How many people walk about with that kind of vitamin deficiency? And here's one: "I have lost the key to my diary." What century was that written in? One glossary I read had the question: "Will you direct me to the frivolity?" That could get you in protective custody in a hurry.

Actually, what this world needs is a universal phrase for "Is the water safe to drink?"

When the exchange of language does not exist, serious charades take over. I have always said if God had meant for us to speak a universal language, He would never have given us ten fingers. When the cook, Ascensión, wanted to know what time we wanted the next meal, she would act like she was feeding herself. I would hold up eight fingers, signifying eight o'clock. When my mother enjoyed the dinner, she would pat her stomach, stick out her tongue a couple of inches, smack her lips, and say, "Yummy, yummy." My mother usually doesn't talk like that.

Ironically, my college Spanish began to come back with an occasional word here and there—usually nouns. Everything was good (*bueno*) because I couldn't think of the word for bad. We did a lot of smiling, bowing, and nodding, and when things really got frustrating, I would burst out, "My younger son is arriving with the verbs. Hang on. He gets here day after tomorrow and things will be better." They had no idea what I was babbling about.

On the morning of the first day at the villa, the housekeeper, Marguerita, came to me and escorted me to the kitchen. She put a very large shopping basket over my arm and pointed to the door. You can't get more graphic than that. I was to buy the food at the town market and Ascensión would cook it.

I gathered the women of our family together

and gave each of them a basket and an assignment. One was to go to the "meat place," one to the bakery, one to the fish house, and one to the stalls of fruit and vegetables that lined the walking street. The instructions were simple: Don't even think of returning to the car with an empty basket!

We did well at pointing out what we wanted. It was only when they wanted to know in Catalan how many or how much that threw us. The merchants were wonderful. They knew we didn't know diddly from squat. After a couple of stressful hours at the market, I plopped down in a chair at the small outdoor cafe at the end of the street and summoned a waiter. "*Uno cabeza,*" I said crisply. The waiter stared at me. I repeated my order.

Turning to my husband I said, "Is it too early to order a beer or what?"

"You want a *cerveza,*" he said. "You have just ordered a head."

"I knew that," I said. "I just wanted a *cabeza* on my *cerveza.*"

The son with the verbs helped.

Four years at USC and finally something was paying off. He could use the phone to confirm our reservations, tell the staff what we wanted to eat, order fresh towels, and get information on tourist sites.

There was no television or radio in the house,

which didn't matter as we wouldn't have been able to understand them anyway. So we were left to our imagination to fill up the evening hours. It had been a long time since we had done that. Someone had the foresight to bring along a game, Trivial Pursuit, and every night we would gather like the Brady Bunch in the library. It has always been my theory that the family that plays together gets on one another's nerves. I have no reason to change my opinion.

I am too impatient to play games. Especially thinking ones. If I don't know the answer to something I say, "I don't know and I don't care" and I pass the die on to the next team. I play games to get them over with. Other people play games to have a good time.

My son was the worst. Every time he got a question, we lost another ten minutes of the game. He contended there was no answer you couldn't come up with if you used logic. Logic took time. Lots of it.

"All right," said my aunt, drawing a card, "for Science and Nature, how many compartments does a cow's stomach have?"

"He doesn't know that," I said. "Pass the die."

"Wait a minute," he said, "give me a chance."

"You know nothing about cows," I insisted.

"You don't know that," he said defensively.

"I know you entered a cow-naming contest when you were seven years old and named the cow Big Bill. You do not know anything about cows."

He went into his hypnotic state and said, "Let's see, a car has one compartment for gloves, a submarine has at least one compartment, a sleeper on a train is a compartment. I say a cow has four."

"Right," chirped my aunt. "Roll again."

It wasn't just me. As the evenings wore on, we all got a little testy from too much togetherness.

One night my mother drew a question. "What bodily function can reach the breakneck speed of two hundred miles an hour?" She answered quickly, "My husband's feet hitting for the bathroom when I pull in the driveway with groceries to unload." My father was not amused. He said if she was so smart, then how come she didn't know how many stars were in Orion's belt. If it had been Joan Collins's belt, she'd have known.

I was angry at my husband because he couldn't remember the answer to "In her book, what does Erma Bombeck say the grass is always greener over?" and all in all, we agreed we had to get out of the villa more.

The upside to being in a home atmosphere is that everyone can pretty much do his own thing. It's probably one of the most relaxing vacations you can plan. By this time, Ascensión and Marguerita were able to tune out all of us, and I kept smiling and Mother kept patting her stomach (which was growing before our eyes) and saying, "Yummy, yummy."

Our sons and their friend left every morning to cruise up and down the Costa Brava shoreline in search of topless beaches. My parents and aunt played cards, and my husband and I climbed over the rocks of our private beach watching the blue waters of the Mediterranean. He did a little fishing from the shore and I needlepointed. One day as we swung down to our familiar spot, we heard voices. They belonged to two totally nude bathers making their way toward the water. For a full five minutes, my husband and I turned to salt.

The naked woman nearest us resumed her way to the water. At one point my husband cleared his throat and I thought he was going to say something, but he didn't.

Finally, she entered the water and swam out to a rock about fifty feet away and stretched out lazily to catch some sun. My husband turned to me and said, "Did you see that! She wasn't wearing shoes. She could have cut her feet to ribbons on these rocks."

"You really are certifiable, aren't you?" I asked after a minute. "Here's a tramp who invades our space and the only thing you see are her tender feet!"

"How do you know she's a tramp?" he asked. "She looks like she has a nice personality."

"She has the personality of a food processor."

"You don't know that either," he charged.

"When you leave an ankle bracelet on in salt water you're not too bright."

"Well, she obviously comes from a good family. Probably military."

"How can you possibly arrive at a revelation like that?"

"Her posture. It's superb."

"Men! I suppose you'd want your son to marry someone with a tattoo of a duck on her hip."

"That wasn't a duck. It was probably a family crest of some kind."

"Right. And Prince Charles has two lions tattooed on his bicep. Why are you so stubborn about this loose woman who cavorts around in the buff?"

"And why are you so vindictive and judgmental about a person you have never seen . . . fully clothed. Frankly, I'd like to see her become a member of our family."

"She steps a foot in this family and I'm outta here," I said, jamming my needlepoint in the bag.

"Is this an ultimatum?"

"You bet your sweet bird it is."

At this point, the other figure, a male nude bather wearing only a wedding ring, jumped into the water and joined our nymph friend on the rock.

My husband said, "Now he's slime."

"It's funny," I said, "he struck me as someone

who would be very kind to his mother."

The iciness between us was still there at dinner. When Marguerita served us the soup I tapped her on the arm and pantomimed taking off all my clothes and pointed to the beach and waved my arms like I was swimming.

"She doesn't understand you," said my aunt.

"Does the word slut have any meaning in your language?" I shouted.

She looked puzzled, then smiled and went to the kitchen. When she returned, she had a picture of the man and woman we had seen on the beach without clothes. She pointed to the woman, then cradled her arms like she was rocking a baby.

"She is telling you those people in the nude are her daughter and son-in-law," said my husband.

I turned to my son, smiled, and said, "Give me a nice noun and a verb . . . quick!"

On the next to the last day at the villa as we summed up our three weeks, it was a miracle we had survived. We had pantomimed our way through Perpignan, France, where we took a day trip. No one in our party spoke a single word of French. We had made it to the bullfights in Barcelona, and every other day we actually looked forward to going to the marketplace where it was more social than necessary.

When we were told the owner of the villa, an Englishman, was due that night, I must admit we were all pretty excited at the prospect of speaking English again.

He invited us for drinks to the guest house where he was holding forth. His first words were, "Well, ahsposeyuvad a raaathaventrous time at the villa?"

We all leaned forward, straining for something we thought we had missed.

"I beg your pardon?"

"I say . . . iopeather . . . you mericansadnuf of ah jolly whatimeto retn."

My God, he talked like "Masterpiece Theatre" on fast forward. None of us had a clue as to what he was saying.

I positioned myself in front of his face and said slowly in a loud voice, "HOW LONG HAVE YOU OWNED THE VILLA?" As he answered, we all nodded and smiled from time to time. Mother grabbed an hors d'oeuvre, rubbed her stomach, smacked her lips, and said, "Yummy, yummy."

Six Worst Arguments on Vacation

A good argument, when conducted properly, takes the time and full attention of two people.

When performed at home, an argument suffers from too many interruptions and outside pressures. The phone rings. Someone is late for work. Children must be fed. Sometimes one party will break in with, "Are you finished? 'Knots Landing' starts in five minutes." You get busy.

On a vacation, however, there are no limitations on how far you can take a disagreement. For most couples it is the most time they have spent together since their honeymoon. Courtesy has given way to time. Some of our better arguments have erupted on foreign soil.

TOPIC: "Why can't you admit you're lost?"
PLACE: Copenhagen, Denmark
LENGTH OF ARGUMENT: Thirty-six hours
HIGHLIGHTS:

"What's with you men? Would hair stop growing on your chest if you asked directions somewhere?"

"I *did* write down the word you gave me at each corner. How was I to know it was the Danish word for 'street'?"

"What do you mean, 'Does anything look familiar'? I just got here, remember. I'm not taking another step until you are sure you know where you're going."

"I don't want to panic you, but our plane leaves in four days. We are going the wrong way. You didn't believe me when I told you the smoke alarm in our kitchen needed batteries either."

"It's hereditary. Your mother couldn't find her way out of a phone booth if you turned her around. I love your mother. I love your whole family. All of you just need to be supervised at all times!"

TOPIC: "Only an idiot jogs here!"
PLACE: African bush in Kenya
LENGTH OF ARGUMENT: Three days

Six Worst Arguments on Vacation

"Was it your intention to bring me to Africa married and send me home a widow? Because if it was I'm going to cash in the insurance policies now, have my entire body lifted, and go straight to the French Riviera."

"If you are not back in two days, we're leaving you here. This is my final word. No one is going to feel sorry for you because you're stupid. We're going to ship your body home and prop it up in the Boston Marathon. It will be hours before people realize you're not moving under your own steam."

"There's danger out there. Don't you realize that? You can't outrun a cheetah doing a twenty-minute mile."

"Honey, I'm only saying these rotten things because I love you and I care about you. I cannot imagine what I would do without you."

"OK, be stubborn. If you break your leg, don't come running to me!"

TOPIC: "I am ready to walk out the door and you have to go to the bathroom. Why am I not surprised?"

PLACE: Europe, Asia, Mideast, South America, South Pacific, Orient, Caribbean, Mediterranean, Mexico, Australia, and every place we've ever visited

LENGTH OF ARGUMENT: Time it takes to go to the bathroom

HIGHLIGHTS:

"I swear you have kidneys the size of lentils."

"I could go too if I thought about it long enough, but I don't want to inconvenience all the people who have to wait for me."

"Why do you think you will never see another bathroom during the next six hours? They're everywhere, you know."

"It's nothing but a habit. You see me going out the door and your mind instantly goes to your biological functions. You are so programmed, you see an open door and run for the bathroom."

"I know what you're doing in there. You're killing time. You have to put the lid down, refold the towels, dry off the soap, replace the washers, alphabetize your toiletries, and look at your teeth."

TOPIC: "What do you mean I don't need a rug?"
PLACE: Athens, Greece
LENGTH OF ARGUMENT: Ongoing today
HIGHLIGHTS:

"I've got arthritis and I don't need that, either. It's not like I'm buying a country."

"I wouldn't dream of asking you to carry it. Just give me my airline ticket and I'll sit on the wing so you won't be embarrassed."

"Hey, you're the one who bought a Vuitton suitcase in Hong Kong for $36 and Vuitton was misspelled. Don't tell me about shopping carefully."

"I am spending my own money on it and am putting it in the hallway. If you want to walk on it, there will be a toll basket at each end. You can either toss in coins each time or you can buy tokens."

"How do I know it will fit? How do I know Wednesday follows Tuesday? I just know it, that's all. If I don't know, who's to know?"

"I heard that! And I could not get the same thing for less at Wal-Mart."

TOPIC: "I am not going scuba diving."

PLACE: St. Thomas

LENGTH OF ARGUMENT: Twelve hours

HIGHLIGHTS:

"I wish I were one of those perfect people who do not have a single fear, but I'm not and that's my final word on the subject."

"If God meant for me to crawl around on the ocean floor, He would have given me anchors for feet."

"Why is it when I don't want to do what you want to do I'm always wrong? You love making me feel inferior, don't you?"

"Every time I've seen a diver on Jacques Cousteau specials, he has fear in his eyes. Enough said. Case closed."

"When I started this trip I said to myself, 'How can I ruin his vacation?' and I answered myself,

'Refuse to go scuba diving with him. That will make him crazy.' You wanta know the truth? I've been planning this for weeks! My final word."

TOPIC: "I never said I'd meet you under the clock."

PLACE: Shanghai, China

LENGTH OF ARGUMENT: Twenty minutes at high volume, two hours in silence

HIGHLIGHTS:

"You misunderstood me, dear. I always return to the bus and you know it."

"There is no need to shout. Everyone on the bus can hear every word."

"Why are you so sensitive? The people applauded when you boarded because you held the bus up for thirty minutes. It was a joke. Can't you take a joke anymore?"

"How could I have said I'd meet you at the clock when I don't know where the clock is?"

"I am sorry you wasted all your shopping time looking for me. I will fill out the necessary papers to have you canonized the minute we get home. Now put a cork in it."

"Aha! I wondered when you'd dig up the Greek rug!"

Death by Drivers

I can't remember which airline it is, but just before their plane docks at the gate, a captain comes on the intercom and announces, "You have just completed the safest part of your trip."

As I contemplate the row of yellow taxis waiting for the deplaning passengers at the curb, I can only nod my head and mumble, "Isn't that the truth?"

Probably the dumbest thing Americans do is to climb inside a car with a perfect stranger and assume he is going to get you where you want to go.

I had a driver once—a Sean Penn Charm School graduate—who got in a shouting match with a bunch of crazies on the San Diego Freeway.

I expected any minute to be looking into the barrel of a cannon.

Another time, my cabdriver actually leaned out of his car window and passed a map to the driver of a limousine so he could circle the exit ramp to my hotel. We were going sixty miles an hour at the time.

But the night I landed in New York alone sort of sums it all up. A guy saw me get my luggage off the carousel, grabbed it out of my hands, and ordered, "I have a car. Follow me."

Erma, the idiot, followed him to the parking lot where he threw my luggage in the trunk and said, "Get in. I'm going to get a few more fares."

"Hold it!" I said. "This is not a regular cab. I want a regular cab and a driver. Give me back my luggage."

He shrugged and obliged.

At the taxi stand, a nice young man got out of his cab, held the door for me, and said, "You going to Manhattan? Here, give me your bag." This was more like it.

I usually like to strike up a conversation with cabbies. It not only gives you a perspective of what the world is thinking about, but I always figure if they know I'm a homeroom mother, they'll think twice about driving recklessly.

This one was a wonderful driver.

"So what did you do before you drove a cab?" I asked.

"I was in the seminary studying to become a priest." His large brown, pious eyes met mine in his rearview mirror.

I think I looked skyward and mouthed silently, "Thank you, God."

"Why did you leave?" I asked.

"They asked me to . . . about the time I heard the voices."

"You heard voices?"

"I shouldn't be telling you this," he said. "They listen to me and then come after me."

"Then by all means don't—"

"One night," he said, getting very excited, "right here on this seat, one of 'them' materialized. I thought I couldn't stand it. My head hurt. I had to stop the car and get out—"

"You don't have to tell me this. . . ."

"They wouldn't let me back in the car again. Do you know what I'm saying?"

"Yes . . . yes I do."

He paused but kept looking at me in the rearview mirror.

Finally, I said brightly, "So, what do you think of Shirley MacLaine's book?"

"She's a phony," he said sharply.

"That was my feeling," I said, nodding my head, not wanting to disagree.

I was in a car with a licensed driver whose elevator was stuck between floors.

I have ridden with Ph.D.'s who have a résumé

in their glove compartment, strung-out druggies, and a limo driver in California who wanted me to help him sell a story describing the night he had Jack Nicholson and Warren Beatty in his car. What a sweetheart.

In Istanbul, we had a cabbie from hell who literally aimed for people in the crosswalk to see how close he could come to hitting them. He steered the car the entire time with the little finger of his right hand inserted into a small elastic loop attached to his steering wheel. He also smelled like a yak in heat.

Crazies and car pollutants are not the worst of it. The most frustrating thing about riding a cab in America is being unable to find a driver who speaks English. I usually climb into a cab driven by Boris Szorgyloklov, who arrived two weeks ago from Odessa, Russia.

The word "hello" is cookie time for Boris. You wonder how it developed that this man came to America and found himself behind the wheel of a Japanese car.

One can only surmise Boris arrived in this country and went straight to a placement bureau where a sociologist gave him a test. At the end, the sociologist said, "You cannot speak a word of English, you have never driven a car in your entire life, you come from a rural community. You are qualified for only one job: driving a cab in New York."

In Los Angeles one afternoon, I climbed into a cab with an Arab driver who could speak only four words, "I am not rich." As he grabbed a $20 bill out of my hand for an eight-minute ride, I taught him three more new words, "I'm getting there."

When cabs are scarce, however, you are often at their mercy. One night in Mexico, a driver jammed six of us into a single cab. A friend of mine straddled the gearshift. At the end of the ride, she crawled out of the front seat. "You OK?" we asked. "Every time he changed gears," she said, "it was a religious experience."

After our rental car experience in Italy, my husband and I talked about engaging a car with a driver. A lot of our friends had done it. Our neighbors, Bob and Judy, said it was wonderful to set your own pace, see only what you want to see, have a flexible schedule, and leave the driving to someone else. They said it's so easy to set up. All you do is make arrangements with your travel agent and be met at the airport by a car and a driver.

Nothing was said about being heavily sedated.

Indonesia

Every country in the world worries about the threat of aggressive neighbors who seek to conquer them. Not to worry. The Russians will do themselves in by drinking too much vodka. The Japanese will smoke themselves to death, the Finns will phase themselves out from arteries clogged with all those dairy fats, and the entire population of Indonesia will eventually die from the traffic. It's just a matter of time.

For a change, both my husband and I were excited about going to Indonesia. Usually we were a house divided on where we were going to go and what we were going to do, but this country offered everything. It had white, sandy beaches; the Ujung Kulon Game Reserve;

Krakatau, the volcano that erupted in 1883, creating the largest explosion ever recorded in the history of the world; plus one of the most unusual cultures in the world. Although the largest religion is Islam, there is a blend of Hinduism, Buddhism, Christianity, and animism throughout the country.

Once you see the drivers in Indonesia, you understand why religion plays such an important part in their lives. After a day as a passenger in a car, I would have worshipped the hotel draperies if I had thought they would protect me from bodily harm.

The first thing we noticed in Jakarta (Java) was the absence of dogs and cats. It didn't take me long to figure out they had probably once roamed this part of the world in great numbers, but one by one they were picked off by Mercedes and Volvos as they tried to cross the street. It brought about their extinction. People were next.

We picked up our guide in Yogyakarta at the hotel. Outside, he introduced us to our driver. This was very unusual, as one man often serves as the driver and the guide.

The driver was young, frail, and said little. He was emotionless, and from time to time he displayed a tic of sorts. His right eye would blink, his head would jerk, and he stretched his neck as if he had on a tight tie.

"We visit the Sultan's Palace," said the guide, smiling. The car shot out of the driveway like the Batmobile in Gotham City.

I'd like to point out here that I am not a nervous passenger. I have survived three teenage drivers: one who used cruise control in downtown traffic at five P.M., one who put on full make-up and finished her homework while driving through a construction area, and another who got a ticket for driving forty-five miles per hour . . . in reverse. But this was unbelievable.

Most of the highways in Indonesia are two lanes. Everyone passes. Everyone. How do they do this? you ask.

There are basically seven modes of transportation in the country. At the slowest and bottom of the spectrum is the horse and carriage, which is exactly what it sounds like. Next is the pedicab. This is a little buggy on two wheels hooked up to a man who pulls it through traffic. The becak or powered tricycle is next, followed by motor scooters, hired cars (and taxis), then trucks, and finally buses.

This is how the pecking order works. Your car passes another car at a speed of fifty or sixty miles per hour. If you meet a motor scooter head-on in the passing lane at the same time, the motor scooter is below you on the scale of size. He has to disappear. Don't ask me where. He just knows that. On the other hand, if you are in a car and meet a truck or a bus, then you must give way.

It's the old game of chicken that has reached state-of-the-art.

All the while our lives are hanging in the balance as our guide is trying to indicate temples and points of interest. I can't take my eyes off the driver.

Every once in a while, the driver engages in a little ritual that is bizarre. As we stop for a light, he tilts his head all the way to his shoulder and then with both hands gives his head a jerk that would have broken a normal spinal column in half.

"Why does he do that?" I asked our guide.

"It relieves the tension," he says. "Actually, he is a very good driver. You are here to relax. Just sit back and enjoy."

It would have taken a lobotomy for me to relax.

I'd like to say that despite the frenzy and the insane passing, I never saw an accident. But that's not true. It was like being in the middle of Demolition Derby. I saw women on bicycles balancing trays of fruit on their heads, only to be forced to hit the ditch and become fruit salad.

I saw an ambulance give way to—you got it— a truck, and in the city it was not unusual to see people sitting on the curb holding bandaged heads while they hauled their vehicles away. But through it all, I never once saw anger, obscene gestures, or exasperation. I never heard shouts or language of any kind . . . only quiet, emotionless resignation.

Over dinner our first night there, our guide kept insisting, "You must relax, miss. How would you like to see Indonesian dancers in Ballet of Ramayana at the theater?"

He was right. I had worn a hole in the floor of the back seat of the car where all day I had jammed on imaginary brakes with my foot. "I'll go back to the hotel and change into something suitable," I said.

I travel with a limited wardrobe, but I always carry one dress for special occasions. This one was all white with a gold belt and sandals. We should have been suspicious we weren't talking Bolshoi when our driver drove like a maniac down dark alleys and came to a stop on a dirt road several feet from the "theater." Actually, it was a tent with the glow of naked light bulbs shining through the canvas. We bought our tickets and stepped inside. Not only was I overdressed, but the performance was undersold. There must have been seven hundred folding chairs distributed around the riser. There were five other people there besides ourselves. I think they were German tourists.

At seven o'clock, the music started and the

graceful dancers glided onto the stage. Our guide leaned over to interpret what was transpiring on stage. "A young man named Jaka Tarub, while hunting birds one day, sees a lovely nymph descending from Heaven to bathe in the forest lake," he whispered. "He hides but watches the nymph Nawangwulan and falls in love with her. Jaka Tarub steals her clothing. He returns to his hiding place and creates a disturbance to frighten Nawangwulan, but she is unable to find her clothing and so cannot return to Heaven. Feeling sad and lonely . . . "

I listened numbly. My eyes felt like balloons filled with water.

At eight-thirty, our guide was still talking nonstop. "When Dasamuka attacks him and forces him to fight, Kala Marica then transforms himself into a Golden Deer to lure Rama and Lesmana away from Sinta so that Dasamuka can kidnap Sinta. The Golden Deer then teases . . . ."

From time to time, my head would fall to my chest and I would jerk it up to hear his voice reciting in a monotone, "In return, Sinta gives her hairpin to Senggana to deliver to Rama. . . ."

I spit on my fingers and rubbed them across my eyeballs. My husband had his head between his legs. His elbows touched the floor. He was comatose. I looked for some kind of compassion from the five other people in the audience.

They were gone. My arm was bruised from where I had pinched myself in an effort to regain consciousness by inflicting pain. "Then the ape tells both ladies to leave and he begins to destroy the garden," the guide droned on. "He breaks loose and sets Alengka on fire, then returns to Pancawait to . . ."

It was after eleven when we fell into the car that took us to our hotel. I slept the entire time. Maybe that was the answer to surviving as a passenger in Indonesia.

As a break in our schedule, we planned a cruise through the Spice Islands. My husband wanted to climb the mountain of cinder-sand and look down into the smoking remains of Krakatau. It was nice to get out of the fast lane and not worry about rites of passage.

When we docked five days later, the captain of the boat said he would be glad to drop several of us off at our hotel. I settled back into the cushions of his car as if I were safe in the hands of Allstate.

The next thing you know we were weaving in and out of traffic like we were competing in time trials at the Indy 500. Suddenly there was a screech of brakes as we stopped for a red light. Then there was a crash from behind and I flew into the seat in front of me. I turned to look at the van behind us. One of the passengers had hit the windshield. An ambulance siren sounded in the distance. The man assured us he was all right.

I bowed my head and said a silent prayer to the patron saint of Indonesian passengers: Our Lady of Valium.

Slides

No one wants to see your slides.

Get that through your head.

Not your parents who gave you life. Not your kids who are insecure and need your approval. Not your priest, minister, or rabbi who are paid to be kind and forgiving. Not even someone whose life you saved in the war who owes you big.

Every amateur photographer who returns from a vacation fantasizes about putting his pictures in "some kind of order" and perhaps showing them at the Y some evening for a minimal price at the door. Some even entertain thoughts of entering their picture of a dog trying to bite the water coming out of a garden hose in some Kodak competition. A few will even go so far as to look up the addresses of *National Geographic* or *Arizona Highways* in the library.

The slides usually end up in shoeboxes in the closet next to a bowling ball. They become the Siberia of Vacations Past. There are only a few occasions when slides can be shown to benefit mankind.

1. Take seven hundred of them to a war and within minutes, everyone will disperse and go home. Most countries consider slides inhumane, but they can be used in confrontations where no peaceful solution is feasible.

2. Slides are effective in isolated areas where kitchen table surgery is sometimes the only option and anesthetic is not available. There have been cases where the patient has only to hear a click and a voice introducing a couple met in a diner and he is out like a light.

3. Police are just beginning to realize the benefits of a tray of slides to pry confessions out of criminals who proclaim their innocence until force is used. The problem is they confess to anything. One man claimed he was responsible for firing the shot that killed Bambi's mother.

4. Sleep labs throughout the country are finding that slides could replace the sleeping

pill. For generations, scientists have been desperate to find an effective sleep remedy for insomniacs that is not habit-forming. Slides fill the bill.

5. Parents are always looking for new ways to get their grown children married and out of the nest. Quite inadvertently one night, a couple showed slides of their trip to Hoover Dam. When they flipped on the lights, their son had gone. This is considered a breakthrough.

6. It is within the realm of possibility that slides may one day replace nuclear power as a bargaining chip to establish peace between nations. If the Soviet Union has thirty thousand slides of Lenin trained toward the United States, then the United States would stockpile fifty thousand slides of Warren G. Harding. Only a fool would fire off that first slide.

Every time my husband has that sly grin on his face and turns off all the lights and pleads, "Tonight's the night," I cringe.

"I do have a headache."

"This will relax you," he whispers.

"Maybe tomorrow."

"No, no, just sit back and. . ."

"Don't make me do this!"

As the slides fall into the slot and the heat of

the celluloid casts a smoky glow over the light on the projector, my eyes begin to glaze over. Then, as if I have taken a prescription drug, my jaw sags, my head eases back onto the pillow, and I sleep . . . the sleep of slides.

Africa

Whenever I thought about Africa, I thought of Joy Adamson, author of Born Free. I visualized her running through tall grass toward the lioness she had raised from a cub before returning it to the wilds, shouting, "Elsa! Elsa!" I always wondered what would happen if she got within bad-breath distance, squinted, and recoiled, "You're not Elsa."

I thought about Ernest Hemingway living in a tent at the foot of Kilimanjaro and Jane Goodall down to the last rubber band for her ponytail sitting on a mountain observing chimpanzees. I thought of Robert Ruark and Stewart Granger and Richard Leakey. But mostly, when I romanticized about that primitive, mysterious continent, I thought about Ava Gardner.

On screen, Ava visited the Africa I wanted to visit—the Africa where you never sweated, your hair stayed curled, and your lipstick remained moist. Where lions were pets, ice cubes reproduced themselves, and you were never afraid to go to the bathroom alone. Where there were fourteen men to every woman and mosquitoes didn't nest in your hairspray.

But alas, Ava's films mirrored the gentle Africa of a half century ago. There was no danger then . . . only a land filled with malaria and uncharted jungles, unfriendly native tribes, wild animals, and cutthroats in search of gold.

The year I went to Africa, I went on a guided tour with eleven amateur photographers on a camera safari. You don't know what fear is until you are out in the bush with eleven shutter-happy hunters who load film and shoot at anything that moves.

These are people who travel with an arsenal. Each photographer on the trip averages six hundred exposures of stills and about two thousand feet of movies. They carry camera bags worth more than the national budgets of all the African nations combined. They keep meticulous logs of what animals they see, where they see them, and what the animals are doing when they are spotted. They sit around campfires at night, sucking the dust off their lenses with rubber bulbs and speaking a language of ASAs and time exposures.

My husband is one of them. He brought a camera to his own wedding. He postponed the birth of our first child because he was "losing his light." He is the kind of man who goes to the Grand Canyon and insists on stopping the car and getting out to take a picture instead of rolling the car window down like everyone else.

As I watch all of these adventurers on the plane, twirling the dials on their lenses, flashing their strobes to see if the batteries are working, and photographing their feet, I know this is not a group to turn your back on.

Secretly, I vow to ignore all of them and create my own Ava Gardner world. In Kenya, I didn't bother to unpack but headed straight for a Nairobi store where they outfitted you in safari clothes. If I was going to feed elephants and romp with small lions, I couldn't run around in pantyhose.

A short drive out of Nairobi, a small row of blue tents came into view. This was more like it. The Africa I dreamed about. It was all there as I had imagined it: the campfire, the directors' chairs, the mosquito netting over the cots, the shovel behind the tent by a sign that read HIPPOS BURY THEIRS . . . YOU BURY YOURS. I hadn't remembered that part.

Any fantasy I had of hanging around the tent

all day with a cooler and a typewriter vanished in the early hours of the first day. These photographers were hell-bent on bagging their limit of photos and nothing was going to stop them. At dawn, we all piled into Land Rovers painted with zebra stripes in pursuit of the animals of Africa.

The tour group was interesting. There was an elderly couple named Dan and Martha who were from a retirement community in Florida. Actually, I never saw Dan and Martha the entire two weeks we were there. They were always huddled under a raincoat that tented both of their bodies. It seems Martha's film was not winding properly and Dan had to open the back of the camera and didn't want to expose the film to light.

Mr. Markey was a retired science teacher who carried a serious German camera. If you took an aspirin, you couldn't operate heavy machinery or Mr. Markey's camera. He slept with it.

The Rosenstads were a kinky couple who only photographed animals mating. They could spot them a half mile away. Both of their heads would shoot up through the sunroof of the Land Rover like a jack-in-the-box as they shouted, "Stop the car! They're doing it!" Since lions in heat mate every ten minutes, Mrs. Rosenstad kept her camcorder running for thirty minutes one afternoon while the rest of us sweltered in the sun.

The only significant thing I remember about Carrie and her husband, Max, was that they wore the same clothes for two weeks. Their five pieces of luggage contained nothing but film and batteries. She found a puff adder snake near her tent one night and shrugged it off. I figured there was only one thing that could strike fear into the hearts of Carrie and Max . . . the horror that they would die and never again see another KODAK FILM SOLD HERE sign.

Tim was a student and a loner. I thought he was a normal person like me when I saw him one day with a Polaroid camera around his neck. I shared with him that I had an Instamatic at home that did everything but heat soup and validate my parking ticket. He looked at me like something that had died. "I use this only to see if I'm getting the right reading on my light." I told him I knew that.

Vern and June Gibbs drove everyone crazy. They didn't take so many pictures as they gave advice. You would have thought he had been sired by Ansel Adams. Every time someone snapped a shot, he shook his head and asked, "What's your ASA? I thought so. I'd be willing to bet my life you're overexposed." At lodges when someone would complain about his camera, he'd get the "Where's your manual?" lecture. Like you're going to lug that around in your shoe bag, right?

This motley assortment seemed to have only two things in common. All had cameras that were extinct before they got them to their cars, and although they were all photographers, not one of them knew how to use any camera other than his own.

Since Max seemed to be such an authority, I asked him one day to snap a picture of my husband and me together. This stunned the entire group as they never had people in their pictures.

Max looked at my husband's camera like it was ticking.

"Where is the viewfinder?" he asked.

"Where do I push?"

"How do you focus it?"

"Where's the light meter?"

My husband spent more time talking to him than he had talking with me on the entire trip.

We grinned and Max snapped the picture. When we got the print back, our heads were cut off.

I had the distinction of being the only camera-dead person on the tour. As we bumped along the corduroy roads of Africa's game reserves, I watched them load, shoot, reload, and shoot again. They prided themselves on not only capturing Africa's animals on film, but saving them from being hunted to extinction by men toting guns. This was true. But I couldn't help wondering how many animals would have heart attacks trying to outrun the Land Rovers and escape to a place where they were safe from prying lenses. How many of them would go deaf from someone beating on a pie pan to lure them out of hiding places or pounding his fists on the side of the Land Rover to get their ears to stand up. How many could hang on to their vision with all those lights flashing in their faces by day and the headlights freezing them in their tracks by night. How long would it be before photographers wouldn't be satisfied to photograph them as they were, but insist they "do something" like tell where they're from, moisten their lips, or show a little leg.

Africa couldn't have been this crowded when Ava was there. I would have remembered. There were lines at the buffet tables at the lodges, busloads of tourists at roadside gift shops, and one day when a female lion was spotted with her cubs, the word went out and within minutes the traffic looked like a police raid on a nude bar.

I was the woman of mystery on the trip. I dressed for dinner. At night I stared for hours at the campfire and was also the only person who did not have a camera around my neck.

One night as I relaxed alone by the dying fire, Tim passed by on his way to Max's tent. He was trying to trade his malaria pills for a roll of Kodachrome ASA 64. He paused before he spoke. "I'm curious. What do you get out of this trip? I don't see how you can come on a camera safari to

Africa and sit there like a portrait with all those animals around just waiting to be shot. Wouldn't you like to go home with a picture of a white rhino for your fireplace or den?"

I smiled. "Africa isn't a place where you have to have a reason to come. I don't want my vision limited by a camera lens. I'm content to eat Africa's dust, sweat in its heat, bask in its silence. I don't have to zoom in on a hippo yawning. It's enough for me to pull up to a water hole at dusk, turn off the motor of the Land Rover, and just sit and watch for hours the parade of animals that come to drink or roll around in the mud to coat and soothe their wounds. Or maybe relax on the deck of a boat on the Zambezi River on a cool African evening and watch crocodiles surface. Africa is a place for adventurers . . . for lovers and romantics. Do you understand what I'm saying?"

There was a long pause before he said, "Get a life" and disappeared in the darkness.

Actually, my being on the trip did serve some purpose. I was a photographer's decoy. This is how it worked. If one of the camera people wanted to take a picture of a park ranger with earlobes to his shoulders, with bones in them, he would get me to stroll within camera range and strike a pose. Then at the last minute, he would swing the camera out of my range and get the picture he really wanted.

One night during our final week in Africa, I was sitting on the veranda in one of the game lodges sipping on something cold. I had tied a yellow scarf around my pith helmet, and, miracle of miracles, my nail polish didn't clash with the khaki safari jacket. I ran my fingers around the rim of the glass, lost in fantasy of the movie *Mogambo* with Clark Gable, Grace Kelly, and Ava.

I was remembering when Grace Kelly decided to take a walk away from the camp compound and Clark Gable, fearing for her safety, ran after her and was so relieved she was safe he forgot she belonged to someone else and they kissed under the brilliant African sky, silhouetted with acacia trees.

I drifted back to reality. The photographers around the table were bragging about the trophies they had shot that day. Collectively they had bagged the rear of one Cape buffalo, the possible tail of the elusive Colobus monkey, three wart hogs, a Massai sheepherder, and three marabou storks eating garbage outside the lodge kitchen.

I said I was returning to my room when Vern shouted to my husband, "You aren't going to let your wife roam out there in the darkness by herself with all that wildlife, are you?" My husband rose. "Of course not," he said. My heart swelled. He motioned to a ranger with a bow and arrow standing near the door to escort me to my quarters.

"Photo opportunity!" yelled June. "Don't miss it." The group scurried like newborn field mice. Cameras appeared and the entire table of photographers twisted viewfinders and adjusted lenses and light meters to capture the ranger with a bow and arrow and Erma in her Banana Republic garb en route to her room.

Later, when the slide was flashed on our home screen, our children were underwhelmed. "Mom doesn't look real happy," said one.

"That's because she's thinking about her poor children sitting at home eating frozen dinners and being culturally deprived."

"That's it!" said the other one. "It's guilt. We could change that, you know. Just take us with you the next time."

It would serve 'em right.

Picking a Date for the Family Trip

How about the first week of summer vacation?

"I can't get a sub for my paper route."

The second week?

"My boss takes his vacation."

Third week?

"Football practice starts."

Fourth week?

"I got tickets for a concert."

Fifth week?

"My dental work cannot be postponed again."

"I have to be here when they paint the house."

Sixth week?

"Bad. Prestons are going out of town. I'm sitting."

Seventh week?

"Who is nuts enough to travel on a holiday weekend?"

Eighth week?

"I'm between paychecks and can't afford it."

Ninth week?

"That won't give me time to get new underwear for everyone."

Tenth week?

"That's our busy month at the drive-in. They'd kill me."

Eleventh week?

"That's when the Cramdens go and they sit our dog."

Twelfth week?

"Too hot."

"Besides, we have school the next morning after we get back."

"I won't have to time to do the laundry."

"Do we have to go?"

"Hold it! This is the date we are all going on a family vacation. No one will be excused for any reason. We are all going to play together and have a fun time or I'm going to break a few heads!"

Rafting Down
the Grand
Canyon

Standing at the south rim of the Grand Canyon, our family looked like an ad for constipation. I had never seen a more surly or unhappy group in my life.

Our daughter was ticked off because it was four in the morning and she didn't want to be there. Her brothers were fighting because one of them was staring at the other one, and my husband didn't know how he could possibly be on a raft on the Colorado River for six days with only a gym bag of clothes. "They expect me to survive with a bathing suit, a pair of shorts, and three pairs of underwear? I pack more clothes than that to go to the bathroom." I was angry because the last thing I told all of them before leaving home was to wear sensible hiking shoes and there they were in thongs that an eight-mile hike on a rocky trail would rip to shreds. Unless, of course, they didn't fall and break their necks first.

We were together all of five minutes before the entire group pushed ahead and left me behind like a bad habit. As I picked my way slowly down the rocky trail to where a raft awaited, I thought a lot about why we were doing this. Our teenagers did not want to be with us. They had made that clear. They wanted to be home working on their book, *Parents Dearest.*

A sharp pain in my right knee got my attention. We should have stopped having children when we had the majority vote. Now it was three to two. That meant they had control of the phone, car radio, and all other lines of communication. They manipulated every aspect of our lives. They literally controlled the budget and the spending. They had the last word on all major decisions. This vacation was the first undemocratic thing we had done in years. Why didn't it feel good? Another pain started in my left knee and I found myself grabbing rocks for support with every step.

About four miles down the trail, the sun was beginning to get through to me. My water supply was gone and my knees were killing me. I crawled into a small cave for shade to contemplate my future . . . if I had one. My toes felt like they were coming through the end of my hiking boots. Surely, the three kids would be saying by this time, "Our mother has stretch marks over ninety percent of her body thanks to us. We're a family. All of you people can go down the river if you want, but we're going back on the trail and rescue our mother who has sacrificed so much for us."

An hour passed before I sensed a vibration of sorts coming from the ground. It turned out to be a string of drag-in mules carrying supplies to the bottom of the canyon. I hitched a ride, thinking somewhere along the way I'd meet my family coming to search for me. Actually, my husband did get worried and brought water, but by this time I was on the back of a mule.

The kids were all on the raft. As I approached, I heard my daughter's mouth. "Mom's always late. She ruins everything."

As I fell over the large rubber pontoon, the captain of the boat said, "You're the first person to ever start down the canyon on foot and end up on her—"

"Shut up and drive," I said tiredly.

People who have never rafted down the Colorado River wonder what it is you do all day for a week on a boat that holds sixteen people.

Mostly, you float down a patch of brown river dwarfed by mile-high canyons of rock on either side. It is one of the most humbling, unforgettable experiences you will ever know as you ease by these stone cathedrals that turn from purples to reds to golds in the afternoon sun. Occasionally, you sweep through rapids of jagged rocks that sometimes drop the boat off into swirling foam for the ride of your life. From time to time you stop and explore caves and waterfalls and spot wild mustangs and burros that stare curiously at these outsiders. A swim in the Colorado is to say hello to hypothermia.

About three days out, a nice woman from Maine asked, "Do you have any children?"

I assured her I did and pointed to the boy lashed in place by ropes on the pontoon as far away from the group as he could get. Another boy was at the opposite end of the boat reading a comic book, and the third child was getting a serious tan. "And your husband?" she queried. I pointed him out.

"Oh my," she exclaimed. "He's the one we see going to the Porta Potti every night in his bathrobe and bedroom slippers. I thought we were supposed to rough it."

"Believe me when I tell you he is suffering." I smiled.

She thought it was wonderful when families were as close as we were.

Every evening when we made camp, the ritual was the same. Everyone was responsible for putting up his own cot under the stars, waiting for the potties to be erected and for a waterfall to become available for showers. I tried to avoid excessive mothering. I really did. One night as I was in the Porta Potti, I heard a large hawk screeching across the sky and the voice of my daughter saying to a friend, "I have to go. I hear my mother calling." I bit my tongue to keep from yelling, "I heard that! You're grounded until you give birth."

My husband had to admit the food was great and the scenery breathtaking, but he was still fighting the primitive facilities. A good day for him was when he found a rock with an indentation in it for his biodegradable soap near a shower/waterfall.

On about the sixth night, we heard rumbles and saw dark clouds gathering ominously above us as we erected our cots. Someone got the bright idea to seek protection from the rain on the ledges of some nearby caves.

"Not me," I said and positioned my cot in a barren patch of desert alone from the group. "There are bats in those caves and I'm not about to have fifty thousand of them part my hair."

My son was humiliated. "Dad," he whined, "Mom's acting weird again. Make her come in the cave like everyone else."

There's something wrong with bats that I

can't put my finger on. They're . . . they're engineered wrong. All wrong. They never stand on their feet like other mammals. They hang out. They always look like they never use a napkin. I hate that. And any mother with nipples in her armpits just isn't thinking. I felt safer in the open desert.

As I looked up at the black sky, I yelled out in the darkness to my husband, "Are you eating something?" (I knew he had brought his food stash.)

"I am eating dried apricots from my survival bag."

"I'm starving."

"You told me you didn't like anything with fur on it."

"You're not going to share, are you?"

My response was his lips smacking in the dark.

I hoped the batteries burned out on his portable electric toothbrush.

On the last day, everyone pitched in and prepared to take everything out of the canyon we had brought in, from the large rubber rafts to a chewing gum wrapper. To the observer, our kids could have been returning from an orphans' picnic.

I did a lot of thinking about our children on that trip—especially about the wisdom of traveling with them.

My conclusion is, you can leave your children endowments, stocks, a moldy fur coat, and the family silverware, but you cannot pass on to them the memories that have contributed immeasurably to your life—your travels. It's a one-owner legacy, the one thing that goes with you when you go.

Parents think a lot about their legacy to their kids. What would they do with their money? One would take up residence in a Tower Records store, another would fill an entire house with cosmetics, and the other would buy a car that would never get any farther than the cement blocks it was hoisted on in the driveway. After that trip, we decided to spend their money for them by showing them the world. Let them amass their own riches.

We're not talking Brady Bunch here. We're a real family . . . remember? In Ireland, the two brothers had an argument over a bicycle, split, and didn't see each other for two weeks. In Hawaii, they learned by saying "Charge it to room 411," they had the power of the universe.

In the African bush, one fell in the Zambezi River that was crawling with hippopotamus. One ran with the bulls through the narrow streets in Pamplona and told me later so I could have a heart attack in leisure.

My husband has me on film running behind a son who is being lifted over a Mexican bay in a parasail, yelling, "Why are you killing your mother?"

Their hotel bedrooms looked like Beirut, they were always the last ones to board the plane, and they used their passports for scratch pads for phone numbers, but somehow we made it.

If we have given them a legacy at all, I hope it is a desire to see the world and meet some of the people with whom they share this planet in peace.

If that were true, I would never again worry that they would end up with nothing.

There were a lot of vacations we took after the Grand Canyon trip . . . vacations that could have made us look better in print. There were rare moments when we actually functioned like a close family. But I chose the raft trip for a reason.

This was the summer of our discontent with one another. We didn't hang out together. We rarely talked or ate with one another. We didn't even seem to need one another. But we survived it. (I gained three pounds and lost four toenails.) But something important was happening to us on this trip that we didn't even realize was happening.

For the first time we could remember, we were a family who gave one another space to be ourselves. We had never done that before. It was as if we all knew that this was the end of a chapter in our lives and the beginning of a new one. The umbilical cord that had bound us together as a unit for nearly two decades was about to be severed. I realized for the first time it was as frightening for our teenagers to contemplate as it was for us as parents. They had been dealing with it with hostility. We had countered with one last rush of superiority.

From that day on, our lives would all turn in different directions. In many ways it was like the Colorado River. It would wind and twist with a promise of a new experience at each turn of the bend. There would be smooth waters for long stretches, then suddenly a patch of rough rapids that would test us and take away our control. It would demand everything we had to hang on and get back on course again.

We had had hours on the trip to think and to observe one another away from stereos, telephones, schedules, friends, and conversations that sounded more like bulletins. What better place than the solitude of a river.

It would be several years before we planned another family vacation. We all had a lot of thinking and growing up to do . . . a lot of things to prove to ourselves. But strangely, this was the trip that we all talk about and remember, the pictures we pore over in family albums. We have never said it to one another, but it was the last summer of the child . . . the last summer of the parents. From that day on, all moved to become contemporaries.

"Let Me Entertain You"

I live in Arizona where tourism is big business.

One night at one of our popular cowboy steak houses, I watched a group of visiting Japanese men. They had watched a shoot-out, visited a saloon, and allowed themselves to be photographed wearing cowboy hats and six-shooters over their hips. When they sat down to dinner, one of them must have ordered his steak well-done, because he was served a dusty boot on a plate. Just as their steak knives were poised over their meat, a waitress came by with a pair of scissors and cut all their neckties in half. They just sat there—not speaking—as she stapled half of their ties to the ceiling with their calling cards.

They had to wonder how we won the war.

Countries are not unlike hosts and hostesses. The first thing they try to do for visitors is to entertain them. Historic sites and cathedrals are a given, but they want to send you home with something you will remember.

I have discovered most guides who want you to have a good time put you on the back of an animal and take your picture. It doesn't matter what kind of an animal: camel, mule, horse, or elephant. Anything, so long as it terrifies the rider.

We aren't in a country twelve hours before we are perched on the back of some beast of burden. We rode mules to the top of Henri Christophe's Citadel in Haiti and mules down narrow paths in Greece's Santorini. On Easter Island, we rode them wild.

If you want to see the enchanted ruins of Petra in Jordan, you barter for a mule the size of a dog with a little wooden saddle and a raggy blanket. At the end of an hour you feel like a wishbone at a Thanksgiving dinner.

Like the Japanese in cowboy hats, guides enjoy nothing better than dressing you up and taking your picture.

In Jordan, my husband was outfitted in Yasir Arafat headgear. He looked like an Irishman wearing a tablecloth. In Zimbabwe, we wore diseased animal skins and danced around a campfire with shields and spears. In Tivoli Gardens in

Copenhagen, we posed as a Viking couple with horns growing out of our heads. And in Australia, I have a picture of a koala bear zonked out of its mind from the eucalyptus leaves hanging around my neck.

Every country comes alive for tourists after dark. New Zealand's Maori dancers stand in front of your face and stick out their tongues like serpents, and you don't know what happiness is until you've sat through a comedy store in Rio where all the jokes are told in Portuguese.

Many countries you visit like to enlighten you on their history with a musical pageant. This happened in Ireland. Normally, it might be the hottest ticket in town. But when you have just flown for eight hours, climbed on a bus, and been fed an eight-course banquet in a castle, it is not high on your list of things to do.

I knew I was in trouble when they opened the presentation with the arrival of the Celts in 300 B.C. I was hoping for something more current, like the visit of John F. Kennedy in 1963.

By the time the Danes pillaged the land in 1014 and the potato crop failed in 1846–47, I had dozed off. I didn't wake up until Padraig Pearse led the final uprising in 1916 and brought independence to the country.

Folk dances are popular. So are cabarets, ballets, and circuses. Inhibitions are thrown to the wind. You'll never see these people again, so you put on a hula skirt and shimmy or stand on stage and yodel with a Swiss band.

I have made an absolute fool of myself in most of the major capitals of the world. I'm a tourist and I act like one.

Every country has its share of comics. At the Folies-Bergère I was sitting near the stage when the emcee leaned over with a blinding spotlight following him and said, "Madame, would you be so kind as to seal this envelope for me?" I stuck out my tongue to lick the flap and he announced loudly, "Ah, I see you are French."

In Istanbul, it was Shecky Abdul. His entire act was to play an international audience by drawing them on the stage and having them set their respective cultures back two hundred years.

One must look upon all of this as a growth experience—performed before people you will never see again.

There's a bar in Cabo San Lucas in Mexico where they string you up by your feet, hoist you into the air, and you hang upside down next to a cardboard marlin who is wearing dark glasses and holding a fishing pole while they snap your picture. You have to ask yourself, "Do I need to have this good a time?"

Antiquity

The big thing to remember about "antiquity" is that it is never found close to the parking lot. I don't care if it's an old monastery, a fort, a ruin, a city, or an old pot, you have to walk a country mile to see it.

I respect history as much as the next person, but to climb eight hundred forty steps to lie on your back and kiss a stone that doesn't kiss you back is not a must-see on my itinerary.

The fact that Americans drag around the world by the busloads to glimpse the past probably has something to do with the youth of our own country. We revere anything older than George Burns.

My husband, a former history teacher, is disposed to read every single sign on every single exhibit in every single museum. If there is a button to activate a voice, he will push it. If there is a guide who will explain how paint dries, he will listen. If there is a mountaintop where he can view Islamic graffiti, he will scale it.

I gave Stonehenge ten minutes.

It's not that I don't respect age. I respect anything that has been through children and is still standing. A mother cannot view the Acropolis without observing that if just once the Athens jousting team had won the city championship, they would have trashed that site in ten minutes and there would be nothing left to see. It's just that you have to pay such exorbitant prices. I didn't mind taking a train ride to see Machu Picchu in Peru, a cable car to visit Masada in Israel, or a cab ride to walk among Jordan's Roman ruins at Gerash. But those are exceptions. Most trips to antiquity are death marches. I spent a half day crawling up a mountain of cinders in Indonesia to do what? To stare into a hole called Krakatau. It looked exactly like the big hole I stared into in Italy called Vesuvius. The problem is I don't see a volcano all year. Then for two weeks, that's all I see, and I get burned out. Same with museums. Same with churches. Same with ruins.

My husband and I do not look for the same things on these trips. He is focused, asks questions about the size of the bricks and the date the cathedral was restored. He maintains a diary of where he has been and what he has seen.

My observations include the IQs of women who wear heels on these excursions, how late the gift shop will remain open, and how do we know if Mary, the mother of God, *really* lived in that house? Did they find monogrammed towels marked BM for Blessed Mother?

I get the feeling that in many countries, especially those in the Mideast, male guides are put off by Western women's assertiveness and independence. They are used to women in a subservient role who wear gray, keep their mouths shut, and hang on to every male word.

Never was it more obvious than our visit to Ephesus, a group of Roman ruins in Turkey. At ten in the morning the temperature was 104 degrees. Our guide was a history buff who never tired of telling long, complicated stories about each rock. The word "menopause" had no meaning for him. Every two minutes he would stop and launch into a long historical harangue in Michener-like fashion, going all the way back to 88 B.C. Somehow he must have sensed that he did not have my complete attention. As he lectured, I was either searching for a restroom or a water fountain. From time to time I would stalk a bird to catch its shade when it landed. As I collapsed on a rock bench in the amphitheater, he said, "I have a story that will interest you." I brightened.

"This is the spot where Artemis-Cybele was worshipped," he said. "They were a group of women who were dedicated warriors—archetypal women's libbers." He paused and his eyes met mine. "These women had sex with men once a year so that the race might not die out. The male children were left to die at birth." He had my attention. "Artemis is always shown as an Amazon," he continued, "one breast bare, the peplum draped over the right shoulder to hide the scar where the other breast had been cut off to allow full freedom for the bow arm." I nodded blankly. "But then you could relate to that." He smiled.

I looked down at my own bust and wondered what he meant by a crack like that. And all that because I opened my own car door.

When the opportunity came up for a trip to Greece, my husband was ecstatic.

"Don't you want to see the site of the first marathon?" he asked. I shook my head.

"Don't you want to see the Temple of Apollo at Delphi where the oracles hung out?" I said no.

"Do you want to die without seeing something older than yourself?"

We got a guide who was right out of central casting. He wore a cap and a scarf under his tweed jacket, and he puffed on a pipe he could never keep lit.

He had a way of demanding your complete attention when he spoke. As we filed on and off buses at each historic site, I felt like I was in the fourth grade on a field trip to a power plant. I was becoming paranoid that everyone on the tour had asked a question except me and he knew it. I knew that one day when I least suspected it, he would glare at me and ask, "You! The one with the Dixie cup of ice! How do you think the excavations at the palace of Knossos, Gortyna, compare with those of Phaistos in the Mesara?"

More than once our eyes had met. We were in Thebes and down to the last day before returning to Athens. The pressure was more than I could bear. My time was running out. There were perhaps thirty of us standing around when there was a silence and he looked straight at me and asked, "Have you no questions?"

He didn't want to hear my real questions. Since I had arrived in Greece, I wondered why all the male nude statues were missing the same sexual biological appendage. What happened to all of them? Were they stored somewhere? Were the museums denied funds until they removed them? Did the militant Amazon women of Turkey hold their convention in Greece? Was it the first thing to crumble? What?

Instead, I said quietly, "Does this lion I'm leaning against have any historical significance?"

Thirty people stiffened in anticipation of what was coming. He glared at me for several seconds before he spoke. Then he said, "You were not paying attention. I told you not two seconds ago it marks Thebes' defeat by Philip of Macedonia in 338."

I mentioned my husband keeps a diary. To show you how crazy Americans can get over antiquity, we were in Spain and someone in the bakery one day mentioned a great old church called St. Lucas. We got in the car and my husband handed me a sheaf of papers from a yellow legal tablet with directions on how to get there. Fasten your seat belts.

Go NW from Palagrugel—C-255 (road to Le
  Bisbal)
About 5 k turn rt. to torrent—3k to dead end
Turn left to pals (14c castle/tower)
Continue on NW plus RV. ter to Torrdella (13
  castle/view)
Return same road to RV ter. Turn rt. at once!
At Serra de Daro turn left to Ullestret (11 c
  church)
Continue on to Vulpellach (14 c castle)
Take Main Rd. rt. W. to Le Bisbal, go left SW
  to Cruilles. 1st rd. to Cassia de la Selva.
  Same direction next rd. turn r. to San

Saduri to Monella (?)
Turn south to S. Sebastian—Then La Franc
(lighthouse) to Callella to Cabo Roig.

A footnote. When we arrived, St. Lucas was
closed. The church was built in 1936. We were
born before that.

Sick

There is nothing more miserable in this world than to arrive in paradise looking like your passport picture.

Yet our doctor will bear us out on this. Our entire medical file is composed of vacation-induced maladies, injuries, and mysterious fevers. We return from a trip sicker than we left. His medical opinion is that if we don't stop relaxing and start staying home, travel will eventually kill us.

Actually, he is probably right. We have paid as much as $300 a day to throw up in a sink shaped like a seashell. I have a history of packing three bathing suits for a trip to the beach and pulling the draperies in my room because I couldn't bear to look at daylight. I lived for a Caribbean cruise to St. Thomas during which you eat eight meals a day, only to wallow in my bunk eating dry crackers and drinking clear liquids.

I don't know what it is—the excitement or the water, the food or the change—but my entire recollection of Santiago, Chile, is lying in a hotel room watching Mr. Ed, the talking horse, spewing out one-liners in Spanish. All I wanted to do was to go home and die in my own bed where maids didn't keep running in and out with clean towels, but my husband said no, "We can't go home. The airline charges $75 a ticket to change the reservation, and you don't want to know what it takes to return a two-week rental car before its time."

I said if he were sick we'd go home, and he said, "That's because when I get sick, I get sicker than you."

Hold that thought. I'd like to tell you about Peru. We were on our way to Machu Picchu and flew into Cuzco where the altitude is eleven thousand feet. It was a landing to take your breath away . . . assuming you had any left. No sooner had we checked into our hotel than we were approached by a waiter carrying two cups of tea with cocaine leaves floating in it. Holy Nancy Reagan! What to do! Before I could "just say no," he assured us it was wise to drink it. It would make us sleepy and as we rested, our bodies could become acclimated to the altitude.

My husband drifted off right away. I, on the other hand, figured I had a few hours of daylight before the gift shops closed. Besides, I could sleep at home.

The next morning my husband could not get out of bed. His flulike symptoms made him headachy and listless. "It's probably just flu," I said.

"My fingernails are turning blue," he said.

"It's probably more than flu," I said. We called the hotel doctor, who flung open the windows, put an oxygen mask on my husband's face, and proclaimed him a victim of altitude sickness.

Between dry, parched lips, he summoned me to come closer to his bed and whispered, "We've come all this way to see Machu Picchu and I don't want you to miss it just because I am at death's door. Don't worry about me being here all by myself in a foreign city where I don't speak the language and am at the mercy of a phone that doesn't work half the time. I want you to board the train and go to Machu Picchu and have a wonderful time."

"OK," I said, and I was out of there.

Later, when we talked of the experience (and God how he talked of it), the concern wasn't that my husband was going to die alone, it was the agony of paying all that money to stare at ugly wallpaper all day.

According to our doctor's log, our journeys

have given us bruised kidneys, blackened toenails that eventually fell off, blurred vision, rashes, pulmonary disorders, chills and fever, conjunctivitis, dehydration from diarrhea, mysterious insect bites that refused to heal, lymph gland infections, sunburned feet from whale watching in the Baja, and a mysterious tropical disease that took six weeks out of my life.

Some illnesses are givens. I know that whenever I am at sea, I can be found at the railing hopefully with the wind at my back. No matter how many precautions I take, I still cannot tolerate the motion of a boat or ship. We had the kids with us one year and decided to cruise out to a little French island called Guadeloupe in the Caribbean.

It was a three-hour trip. The boat had two classes: first and tourist. My husband announced, "Kids, I think your mother would be more comfortable in first class. Maybe there wouldn't be so much motion. I know you're saving money, so you can go tourist if you like."

Well, you would not believe the jokes that ensued. "Mom can't be classless for three hours? What does she think we're going to do in tourist? Ride next to live chickens? Who's going to take her place at the oars?"

I ignored them and we paid the extra thirty bucks to sit in an air-conditioned cabin with soft seats and a TV set. The classes were divided by a curtain.

Five minutes away from the dock, I grabbed two barf bags and hit the floor, flat on my back. It was not a pretty sight. Hearing laughter, I looked up, and standing over my chilled, sweating, nauseous, green body were the kids. "So this is first class," they chirped. "Nice seat you got, Mom. Too bad you're missing an old 'Perry Mason' rerun on your TV set."

If the environment doesn't get you and the water doesn't do you in, you have one last obstacle to clear before you can come home well: food.

You have no idea what you are eating. One day in Africa, we were having a box lunch. As I picked up a piece of meat, I asked, "Does anyone know what kind of an animal has a one-and-a-half-inch thigh?" Everyone stopped eating, returned the meat to the box, and hit for the fruit.

Travelers feel the world is so homogenized that there is no place they can go without getting American food. This isn't really true. I could hardly wait until we got to Israel to sample all that New York deli cuisine—you know, the sandwiches with two pounds of pastrami between the softest rye bread on the planet with dollops of hot mustard and a crisp kosher pickle on the side. Forget it. Israel is a whole lamb on a rotisserie dripping fat in the restaurant window, hummus made out of chickpeas, falafel, and tasteless bagels the size of hubcaps.

Most countries use very little meat in their diets. They serve a lot of fish. I have the feeling that I am eating bait most of the time.

And it works in reverse. Can you imagine what Fatburgers look like to a man from New Delhi? I was seated on a plane next to a man from Japan one day when lunch was served. He didn't speak a word of English, so there was no warning him when he picked up his knife and fork and began to saw through a large, firm pat of butter. He properly balanced a bite of it on the fork, deposited it in his mouth, and began to chew slowly.

Throughout the years, I have set up my own rules for eating (or not eating) food:

Never eat anything you can't pronounce.
Beware of food that is described as, "Some
    Americans say it tastes like chicken."
If a country does not have one single head of
    cattle, no ranges, and no cowboys, don't
    order beef.
This is no time to be a sport. When they tell
    you the skin of what you are eating makes
    wonderful shoes and handbags, leave it.
Resist eating anything that when dropped
    on the floor excites a dog.
In countries where men wear red checkered
    tablecloths on their heads, don't order
    Italian.

Someone did a survey on the number of travelers who suffered from some physical ailment while traveling. It seems sixty-two percent of vacationers come down with upset stomachs, heartburn, indigestion, diarrhea, and sunburn.

Sometimes it's carelessness. Other times you have only to mention one word that will bring you to your knees . . . MEXICO!

Mexico

My young son and I lay side by side on the double bed with all the curtains drawn, casting the casita into darkness.

The door opened and a blinding ray of sunlight caused me to grab a wet towel off the nightstand and cover my eyes, and him to bury his head in the pillow.

"Why don't you come to the beach?" asked my husband brightly. "It's beautiful!"

"How far is it from this room?"

"Twenty . . . thirty yards, max."

"That's too far from the bathroom," I groaned. "Shut the door."

"What about you, sport? I thought you wanted to go parasailing?"

My son threw a pillow at the door just before it slammed.

We had been in Mazatlán only an hour or so when both of us were struck down with Montezuma's revenge.

Forget the fact that I would go home looking like I had been bled white by leeches. Forget lazy days on the beach and romantic nights listening to strolling mariachis. Forget that two dollars would buy me the leather coat of my dreams. I was stuck for a week in this dark room watching cartoons of Tom and Jerry chase each other, with Spanish subtitles.

My mother, who was also on the trip with my father, poked her head in the door. "Bill tells me you want to stay in this depressing room all day. You missed a wonderful lunch. I had a cheese crisp and a large salad."

"Mother, you're not supposed to eat the lettuce or the tomatoes."

"I don't believe all that nonsense. Here, I brought you both a bag of tortilla chips from the dining room. Be careful. They're greasy."

The bag landed on the bed between my son and me. It took only a few seconds for the odor of the animal fat to reach our nostrils before we both bolted to the bathroom.

"Are we bonding yet?" he said, raising his head weakly.

"Any minute now," I said.

A commercial that I had seen on television came to mind. It showed a Hispanic family who were at Disneyland eating hot dogs and cotton candy. They were holding their stomachs and looking miserable. Then a pink substance oozed down over the screen. When it cleared, the family was smiling and saying, "*Gracias* Kaopectate." I used to think about that commercial a lot. Was it possible that people coming to our country couldn't drink the water and suffered stomach cramps during their entire stay? I wanted to believe that.

I love Mexico. It is our Arizona neighbor, and every chance I get I whip across the border at Nogales and poke through the richness of its creativity. I'm there maybe four or five hours before I begin to dehydrate and I must reenter the United States for a drink of water.

It's funny about water. When I am home I have to force myself to drink three glasses a day. When it costs $1.49 a bottle, I am like a sponge.

A friend of ours rented a house one summer in San Miguel de Allende. I made up my mind I was going to be super-careful. I rinsed out my toothbrush in bottled water. I shut my eyes and closed my lips while showering so that not a drop of water invaded my temple of fluoride.

We boiled large tubs of water and used it to make coffee. We washed and rinsed our dishes in boiled water. At a pharmacy we bought a special chemical to soak fresh fruits and vegetables to kill off anything that might infest our system. I chewed so many Pepto-Bismol tablets my teeth turned pink.

One day my husband asked, "Want to go for a swim?"

"How far is the pool from the house?"

"Fifteen . . . twenty yards tops."

"That's too far," I said.

There are some people who have stomachs of iron. They can drink water from the tap, eat street food, and feel nothing. My mother is one of those people. She'll try anything. She's the only one I know who leaves an airline and says to the stewardess, "Compliments to the chef."

I remember when we returned from Mazatlán she dropped off at the drugstore to get something for her constipation.

Is that sick or what!

Traveling with Parents

Several years ago when I was a roving correspondent for ABC's "Good Morning America," I traveled to the Grand Canyon to do a story on the lack of facilities in national parks to accommodate the handicapped. The parks belong to everyone, and being limited by crutches or wheelchairs should in no way diminish the enjoyment or appreciation of the surroundings.

To prove the point, I sat on a ledge of the canyon with a young blind man from Northern Arizona University, Flagstaff. I asked him what he "saw" on his descent into the canyon.

My eyes were wet with tears as he described hugging the large boulders that held the heat of the sun long after it had gone down. He told of how he heard giant hawks overhead and felt the coolness of their shadows. From the echoes, he gleaned the scope and depth of the canyon. He felt the winds stir the brush along the trail and scooped up the cold water of the restless Colorado that carved out a place for itself on the canyon floor. He even felt the layers of rock that left their own imprint of time and glacier activity.

When he finished, I vowed that never again would I believe that people are too old or too incapacitated to travel and to enjoy where they are.

When my parents were younger, they traveled a lot. Later in their lives, when my father had difficulty in getting around, they announced their traveling days were over.

I thought they were too young to retire their passports and told them so. Why should they get to sit at home and live the good life while the rest of us were out there kicking suitcases in a checkout line, climbing on and off tour buses, filling out landing forms, and struggling with language. Besides, we had seen too many older people on our travels climbing over rocks, riding camels, scaling mountains, and putting in fifteen-hour days to know that if you really wanted to see the world, it was doable.

My mother said it would be nice to travel with us, but we should pick a nice, easy vacation so they could keep up. Something not too weird that would challenge us but still be relaxing for them.

"I was hoping you'd say that," I said.

"So where are we going?"

"Down the Amazon."

Now, before every amateur traveler in the world rushes out and plans a vacation with parents, you must ask yourself a few questions and answer them honestly.

1. Did your mother-in-law wear a black arm-band to the wedding?
2. Do they still think Hawaii is a foreign country?
3. Are you still arguing with your mother over whether a three-year-old should have a pacifier implant?
4. Do your parents tell you to sit up straight and not talk with food in your mouth?
5. Do you have anything in common beyond occupying the planet Earth?

Happily, the four of us genuinely like one another and travel well together.

We flew to Manaus where the dark waters of Brazil's Rio Negro meet the muddy waters of the Rio Solimões to form the Amazon. Then we transferred to a canoe where we eased our way through cocoa trees, rubber plantations, and channels of tropical birds and huge water lilies. Actually, the pace was pretty leisurely, but back in the city my dad ran out of gas. Shopping to him was on the same social plateau as mud wrestling. He said, "I'll wait for you here on the park bench. Take your time." Thus began my father's own private adventures. From that moment, his vacation took on a life of its own. As he whiled away his afternoons on the bench, he was entertained by a snake charmer, treated to a political debate, and hit on by two hookers.

In every city we visited, on every trip we took, he staked out a spot in the center of town and absorbed the sights and sounds of its people. If we wanted to know what was going on, we asked him.

He wanted desperately to see the large statue of Christ the Redeemer that rises one hundred feet into the air on a peak overlooking Rio. But the train only took us part of the way up. The rest you had to walk. That was difficult for him.

It took both of us an hour and a half to make it to the top, but it was a personal triumph for him, as was the entire trip. He and my mother display the proof of their efforts on their kitchen wall. They had their picture taken and mounted on the tackiest plate in South America. They paid $15 for it. It's worth a million in memories.

Vacations are nothing more than a series of "moments." These are special times that you remember in between all the exhaustion of getting from one place to another. That trip with my parents was to be the beginning of a lot of trips we took together. It was also a time of discovery. We were seeing one another as friends.

I discovered my mother could carry on a conversation with a street sign. She never knew a stranger. One day on a boat trip outside Rio, she was "chatting" with a family from Argentina. Mom had a bandanna over her mouth and two imaginary six-shooters in her hands, and they were nodding like they understood what she was saying. I can only assume she was telling them she was from Arizona, home of cowboys and Indians. Then again, she could have been telling them about a bad meal she got in Rio where the owner overcharged and she felt like wasting him. Who knows?

In Ireland, my father never really understood how bed-and-breakfast works. When we pulled the car into the driveway of a private home, he said, "I don't want to bother these people. Let's go to a hotel." We tried to explain to him what he suggested was a lot like checking into a Marriott and saying, "Look, if you're busy, we'll just sleep in the car and eat a candy bar."

"That's what these people do for a living," I explained. "They want guests. Look at them. They're coming out to the car to meet us, and they're smiling."

He still wasn't convinced. He went into his bedroom and didn't come out until we loaded up the car in the morning. Then he apologized to them for dirtying two towels. So much for culture exchange.

One day in Spain, I said to them, "How would you like to see a bullfight in Barcelona?"

"I've seen it on TV," said my dad. "It's too bloody."

"You love Ava Gardner, don't you?"

"Yes."

"Ava Gardner loved bullfights."

"She did?"

"Never missed them," I said.

"We could possibly last through one," he said.

Actually, there were six bulls to be fought that day, and like the child who eventually turns into the mother, I got them settled and gave them their instructions. "You have to understand, this is a national pastime in this country, and they do not view it with the same horror or disdain as Americans do. We have to respect that. All I'm asking is that you refrain from making comments about 'What kind of animals are these people?' and 'How would they like it if bulls in capes stuck spears in their necks?' OK?"

They nodded their heads in agreement.

When the first bull was released, Mother said aloud, "You poor thing. If you knew what I know."

"Mother!" I snapped.

"Sorry," she said.

When an ear was presented to a woman in a box just down from us, my father shook his head from side to side.

"All the meat goes to the orphanage," I said, patting his hand.

For the next five encounters, we heard absolutely nothing from either of them. Not a peep. When I turned around to tell them it was time to go, both were sitting there with their eyes closed.

You never dwell on what you can't do on a vacation, but what you can do. My dad didn't have to play St. Andrews golf course in Scotland. Seeing it was enough. He didn't have to roam the Cliffs of Moher in Ireland. It was enough to feel the mist on his face and watch the birds dart in and out. Just sitting around on park benches, parking lots, walls, and sidewalk cafes, he probably absorbed more of the flavor of the country than we did.

It is important to note my dad didn't snap a single picture. He didn't have to. His memory was an album of moments he cherished till the day he died.

Restrooms

In 1984, I traveled to NASA in Houston to do a piece on the space shuttle for "Good Morning America." If this was to be the Greyhound bus of the future, I had to know the most important thing about it: "Where's the toilet?"

This probably seems insignificant to most people, but as far as I'm concerned, plumbing is the key to world power. It is the universal language, the one essential that binds us all together, the common denominator that is of the utmost importance to those of us who share this planet.

One cannot possibly imagine the prestige that will be accorded the nation who perfects a toilet that works. Toilets were invented by the

Romans in the second century. The very next day, Out of Order signs were invented.

At NASA, a public relations man directed me to a large seat in the space capsule that looked like a death chair. It had a seat belt and head and foot restraints to compensate for weightlessness in space.

"This is the space toilet," he said.

"Does this really work?" I asked.

"Not well," he said reluctantly. "We've got a lot of bugs to work out."

Five years of research and $12 million worth of engineering had gone into this mechanism, and it still didn't function properly.

I'd like the adventure of going to other planets as well as the next person, but until they can either come up with a toilet that functions or a plumber who works in space on Sundays, I'm not going.

Istanbul

Istanbul is a city in Turkey shrouded in mystery, steeped in history, rich in antiquity, and stubbornly hanging on to its old-world ambience. And that's only the toilets.

Restroom facilities aren't as important to men as they are to women. Male travelers tend to focus on ruins that have withstood time, palaces that harbor secrets, and religious shrines that have shaped the destiny of a country.

Women might be interested in all this too if they had the time. But they have to figure out if you pull a chain to flush, step on a pedal, push a button, jiggle a handle, or push a detonator on the back of the commode like you are blowing up a train.

Istanbul is the ultimate restroom experience. I hardly know where to begin. I'll start with my back. Due to a herniated disk, I was in bed for four months before I embarked on the trip. This is important for you to know because it explains why my leg muscles were gone.

Leg muscles are absolutely essential in Istanbul because all of the restroom facilities are nothing more than a hole in the floor with two little Arthur Murray feet etched in the cement on either side of the hole facing a wall. There is nothing to hang on to. Once you're down there, you've made a serious commitment.

You don't know despair until you have fallen on your backside on a (ugh) wet restroom floor in Istanbul with your English cries for help falling on Turkish ears.

For years, I have been waiting for a travel writer with the courage to put out a handbook (waterproof, of course) telling us what to expect in the way of restroom facilities. They all tap dance around the subject like it's not important. To women, it's right up there with breathing and a valid passport.

We should know if they're called loos or WCs. We should know whether we have to carry our own tissue, which ones are unisex, and how much money they cost before we can use them.

If I had been enlightened, I would never have asked a man at the gas station in a small village in

Africa if he would give me the key to the restroom.

He looked at me like I had just asked for the keys to the kingdom of heaven. Instead, he laughed and pointed to the bush surrounding us. I declined.

A few miles from the station, I asked our driver to pull over to the side of the road. As I slid back the door he warned, "Watch out for lion in the ditches. They like to sleep there."

I hesitated. "Oh, and if you pick a tree," he added, "look up and make sure there is nothing in it."

If someone had told me a week before that I would ask a man I had known for only twelve hours to accompany me to the bathroom, I would have said he was crazy.

I'm not suggesting restrooms in the United States are exactly models for the world. Most of the facilities abroad bear two initials: WC for water closet. You can figure that out. But can you imagine a foreigner coming to our country and trying to figure out the little symbols we use on restroom doors? Even I have trouble with them. There are Senors—Senoritas, Messieurs—Mesdames, Cowboys—Cowgirls, Chiefs—Squaws, Tarzan—Jane.

They get more creative than that. There are pointers and setters, Samson and Delilah, Romeo and Juliet, Scarlett and Rhett.

Ever since my husband found me, sans glasses, with my nose pressed against a restroom door following the outline of a little figure in a hooped skirt with my fingers and asking if that was a skirt or a man wearing a cape, he cases the place first.

I hate the ones named after animals. I'm not good with animals. I'm OK with heifers and steers, stallions and mares, chicks and chicklets. But one night I didn't know the difference between a ram and a ewe. We can never go back to that restaurant again.

At least most American restrooms are free. Many foreign restrooms are not.

In Istanbul, every restroom is guarded by a little old man sitting at a card table who charges you a minimum of 100 lire (about 15 cents) to use an open pit with no paper, no towels, no soap, and no deep breathing.

Recently, I read a story that the Soviets in their move toward capitalism installed their first pay toilet in Moscow not far from Red Square at a charge of 10 kopeks (about 3 cents). That's not a capitalistic moneymaker. Capitalists aren't that cruel or that stupid. You show me a pay toilet in the United States and I will show you a woman in Donna Karan slacks crawling on her stomach under the door to avoid paying 10 cents.

Recently, a couple who were going abroad for the first time visited us. My husband smiled and said, "What luck! Erma keeps a diary. She can probably give you some suggestions on what to see."

"We'll land in London," the woman chirped.

I flipped through my notes. "They're called loos, dear. Have chain flushes. Take your own tissue. Will you hit Germany? The restroom by the Rhine was adequate. Roller towel was quite soiled. The one in the department store in West Berlin, however—"

"What have you got on the Eiffel Tower?" she asked, moving closer.

"The Eiffel Tower restroom had soap and tissue, but the lines could throw you into kidney failure. Switzerland had sparkling mirrors and the locks were secure on the doors."

"Is it true what they say about Italy?"

"Every word,' I said.' "No paper, graffiti . . ."

The men just stared at us. To them, it's a place to whip in and out. To women, it's half a day out of their lives standing in line and wrestling with cumbersome clothes. It's funny, but men don't question why at public events women have never heard an overture, never seen a curtain rise on the second act, never heard the *Star-Spangled Banner*, never had the luxury of finding their seats with the lights on. What do they think we do in there? Kill time?

We spent a week in Istanbul, a city that is half Asian, half European. On our return, my husband regaled friends with his boat trip down the

Bosphorus, his visit to the Blue Mosque, St. Sophia, and the spice bazaars.

I am still talking about the white marble baroque palace of Dolmabahce. With all that money, don't you think the sultan could have sprung for a real sit-down toilet?

Brochure Speak

Some of the most creative fiction being written today are travel brochures. They rank right up there with Michener and Ludlum.

"Tonight, sit back and enjoy a romantic gondola ride in Venice." It's the dream that torments and eventually seduces those of us in bumper-to-bumper traffic each morning, drinking coffee out of a foam cup.

We live the fantasy of lying in a boat in the arms of our husbands (who look twenty years younger in the dark) while a gondolier with the voice of Placido Domingo serenades us. There is never a clue that this is the summer when tourists and gondoliers wear face masks to filter out the smell of rotting weeds and polluting algae that kill fish and create an odor that could turn off a nymphomaniac.

In brochures, the motorcoach is always a "luxury" motorcoach, all hotel rooms overlook the bay, large terrace, and gardens, and every restaurant has "old-world ambience."

The following are phrases that have appeared in travel literature that we bought . . . literally.

"Spacious suites to enjoy as you cruise the Norwegian fjords"

This is accompanied by a picture of a woman in an evening dress sitting at a small table while her husband in a tuxedo pours her a glass of champagne. What the picture doesn't indicate is that they have to hoist the table on the sofa before they can open the door, he is sitting on the toilet seat lid, the room is below the water line, the curtains cover a wall, and they are both trolls.

"Bring extra film to photograph the last remaining Javan rhino recorded by Marco Polo, wild boars, tigers, leaf monkeys, and two hundred species of birds"

Promises, promises. I let a domestic cow slip right out of my camera range. That's too bad because it was the only animal I saw.

"One could easily spend several days visiting the more than eighty-six thousand items on display in the museum"

Which is too bad because the bus will stop for only twenty minutes.

"Latin Americans do not have the same sense of urgency that we from the Northern Hemisphere feel"

Set your alarm for dinner.

"The phrase for 'Bring me drinking water, please' is *Lete maji ya tafadhali kunyua*"

If I could remember that, I'd be smart enough not to drink the water.

"Leisure afternoon to shop"

This is a contradiction in terms. Shopping is work if you do it right.

"Food for the adventurous"

I could stay home for that.

"Never swim alone if you suspect the presence of sharks"

So what do you do? Buy a friend?

The pitches I really love are the ones that say their tour excursions "aren't for everyone." There was one ad that offered sixteen days in Zimbabwe on a rhino reconnaissance safari. Another adventure in a brochure read, "White-water rafting on the powerful Zambezi River directly under the spectacular Victoria Falls. Looping low figure eights in a small aircraft over the great gorge to photograph myriad rainbows shining through the mist also available."

For nearly a year, my husband pored through a brochure of a fishing and wildlife expedition to

Alaska. We were going to cruise along with an escort of humpback whales. We were going to see the breeding grounds for fur seals and visit islands rich in waterfowl. Giant king and sockeye salmon would jump in the boat, and bears and moose would line the shores and wave as we cruised by.

He was like a kid who couldn't wait for Christmas.

My eyes kept falling on an ominous "Please note" in small print in the back of the brochure. It read, "Due to the unique areas visited on this expedition, changes in the itinerary may be made where necessary or deemed advisable for the comfort and well-being of the passengers. Your expedition director is a professional in travel and will ensure that the best alternative is arranged if a change is necessary."

I got a chill every time I read it.

Alaska

In many ways our salmon fishing expedition in the Bering Sea was a lot like the Broadway production of Josh Logan's Mister Roberts.

The ship sailed from oblivion to tedium with stop-offs at boredom and monotony, the passengers were always five minutes away from mutiny, and the captain actually had a palm tree on the deck outside his door.

Two big differences. The ship was considerably newer than the mythical Navy bucket, the USS *Reluctant,* and when expedition passengers were "bad" they were threatened with shore leave.

My husband, Mister Roberts, booked us passage

on the ship because the very word "expedition" made him crazy. He fantasized he was Marlin Perkins sedating a rhino with a dart gun from a helicopter. In his dreams he became Jacques Cousteau pinned by the winds against the bow of the *Calypso* cruising into Tahiti. When he really hallucinated, he was Robert Redford between the sheets with Meryl Streep.

My first reaction was that I'd pass this vacation up. "Don't be ridiculous," he said. "You don't have to fish. You could join the wildlife explorers or the flora and fauna team."

"They sound like vaudeville acts," I said.

"Trust me on this one, you are going to have the time of your life. We're not talking a smelly fishing boat here. This is a luxury ship with an exercise room, great cuisine, and whole unstructured days for relaxation."

On the day our matching red parkas with the insignia on them, the fanny packs, the caps with the bills, and the boots arrived, I thought he was going to pass out from excitement.

I looked at myself in the mirror wearing the full expedition costume. I could barely stand up, let alone move. From the rear, I looked like a Disney parking lot. Ensign Pulver lives.

The trip was doomed from day one. In all fairness, it really wasn't the fault of the organization that gale winds prevented us from boarding the ship at Nome. The residents there opened their hearts and their homes, and even provided tour buses so we could see Nome's only tree barely standing in the winds. The next morning we were bused to Teller.

The ship was anchored offshore and pitched so badly we were literally pulled from the zodiacs and dragged aboard. Social amenities were not exchanged the first night. We all had our heads in the toilets being ill. Over the intercom we were informed that a lifeboat drill would take place in five minutes. Three people showed up. I was not one of them. The doctor was so sick he gave himself only half a shot in the hip so he could still function. Seasickness patches in the backs of the ears could have been costume jewelry for all the good they did.

There was no one upright for the captain to welcome at dinner the first night.

Early the next morning as we still clung to our beds, the intercom made an important announcement. Since so many of us had missed the lifeboat drill the day before, we were advised that any time we heard five bells, it would be a signal to grab for the life jacket and prepare to evacuate ship.

On day two, all of us crawled from our cabins and made a stab at social interaction. It wasn't easy. The ship was literally divided into three distinct interest groups. The wildlife people had binoculars draped around their necks and carried notebooks everywhere. One man told of how he went without his lunch for three years to save enough money to watch a frigate bird perform his courtship ritual. (I worried when they gave him a steak knife.)

The flora and fauna group lugged around cameras with lenses the size of cannons. In their backpacks, they carried coffee-table volumes devoted to flowers and trees.

The fishermen had hooks sticking in their hats and compared lures like little boys with frogs in their pockets.

The brochure had made promises to all three groups. The wildlifers had been promised a plethora of animals: whale, sea otter, and bear sightings. The nature people were along to tramp through rain forest and stalk the Alaska coastline. The fishermen had been guaranteed they would catch more salmon than they could possibly eat in a lifetime.

I have never seen people so driven to their respective special interests in my entire life. At the mere mention of the words "whale sighting," the dining room would empty and the boat would list to one side. From morning until night, groups gathered in darkened rooms to watch slides of sea lions mating. At breakfast, they filled notebooks with drawings of Indian petroglyphs, and in the lounge at night the sportsmen listened enraptured as diaries of fishing excursions were read.

Every minute of the day, one group or another was being launched in zodiacs to visit a seal rookery, throw in a line, or turn over rocks somewhere.

Have you any idea what it is like to be the only shallow person in the midst of all this? A woman who looked through binoculars and saw only her own eyelash? Who thought that Dolly Varden was a country-and-western singer and that a dark-eyed junco was a description of one of the passengers?

But the sad part about it was that no one was seeing animals, no one was being dazzled by nature's paintbrush, and no one was catching fish. It was as if we were adrift in the twilight zone in a survival experiment.

On the morning of the third or fourth day, I went in search of the exercise room. Following directions from a member of the crew, I cautiously pushed open a small door marked Exercise. There were wall-to-wall mattresses. Two bare-chested crew members, awakened from a sound sleep, snapped, "Whatya want?" I silently closed the door.

That episode brought the Ensign Pulver in me to life. I said to my husband, "Do you know what I am going to do? I'm going to march right into the captain's quarters and push this brochure up his nose and say, 'Listen up, mister . . .'"

"You're not going to do that," said my husband

gently. "Besides, if you have a complaint, get in line behind Mrs. Syckle, who hasn't stopped screaming 'I want to see bear!' ever since she boarded this ship. There's a mutiny underfoot to get rid of the fishing guide, and Joan had the captain backed against a fire extinguisher this morning. All I heard was 'No, you don't understand. I spent all of my alimony on this trip!' These are not happy campers."

One day when I was in my bunk reading, I heard bells . . . five of them. My reaction surprised even me. I felt relief and said to myself, "Thank God, we're sinking." Grabbing my life jacket, I opened the door to see the first officer tearing by. At that moment, the safety doors just outside our room banged shut with an echo of finality, preventing him from passage. He turned directions to race for another exit.

"Are we evacuating ship?" I yelled after him.

"I hope not," he shouted back.

Disappointed, I fell back into bed. It was that kind of a day.

An announcement was made later that someone had been smoking in the exercise room (how's that for irony?) and set off the smoke alarm that triggered the bells to abandon ship. It was my last hope of getting off alive.

It soon became evident that other than the breathtaking views that surrounded us, the riches of Alaska were making themselves invisible to us. At the Iliasi Pass, we were promised a peek at fresh lava flows . . . if the weather was clear. It wasn't. We were teased with a chance to buy Tlingit art at a museum in Klawock. It was closed. We were to tour Cordova for a view of the Million Dollar Bridge. Two hundred and fifty thousand dollars of it had been carried away by moving glaciers. By the hour, the fishermen became more surly and the nature people more moody. The flora and fauna people began to drink.

Every morning when we met for briefings, it was like ninety siblings who all should have been an only child. On about the twelfth day, the leader announced, "We'll drop off the fishermen at 1430. At 1600 we'll combine the other two groups to tour a totem park and a fish hatchery. There will also be a performance of traditional dancing."

That was agreeable to the nature people, but the wildlife people became quite ugly. They were promised a film on the Kittiwake Rookeries, which seemed to settle them down. However, when the fishermen were picked up at 1930 and still had not caught fish, the resource person for fishing was fired on the spot. These people played hardball.

"Where is he?" I asked my husband.

"Gone."

"But we're out on open seas in the middle of

nowhere." I could only assume he was set adrift on a floating iceberg because we never saw him again.

I hung out with all three groups. I sat in a zodiac in a cold rain for three hours and watched a brown spot on shore that half of the group said was a black bear. The other half said it was a tree stump. When it didn't move for three hours, I changed my vote to the tree stump theory.

I found the bird people to be quite extraordinary. Some of them kept track of the number of birds they spotted. I calculate I saw more in an hour from the fantail of the ship following the garbage than they did in two weeks. One day one of them was quite excited about a dark bird with a seven-foot wingspan. It turned out to be a mosquito.

I guess my favorite group would have to be the fishermen. You have to admire these people who are willing to go the distance for their sport. They'd sit around the table and spin stories of how they could taste the salmon they were going to catch in the months to come. My only experience with fishermen had been on the early Saturday morning television shows. There was always some guy named Bubba standing up in the boat with not another single boat around him. He had a friend named Roy who talked constantly and would say things like, "I never kissed a fish with bad breath, did you, Bubba?" And they'd laugh. Every time their lines hit the water, they got a strike. Every time.

It wasn't like that for the fishermen in Alaska. They would sit in the boat for hours at a time. One day one of the men got a hook caught in his lip. I would have been air-evac'ed under heavy sedation to the Mayo Clinic for a week. Not him. He just reached up and said to his wife, "Give me a hand with this, Bev."

One morning as my husband pulled on his fishing boots he said, "What are you going to do at Cordova?"

"I think I'm going with the A group and watch glaciers calve (I have no idea what that is) from the Million Dollar Bridge. On the other hand, the B group is going to tour a salmon sonar counter station."

"Why don't you come with the C group? We're going trout fishing and maybe have a bear sighting at Clear Creek."

"Someone said the A group is hiking McKiley Lake Trail and will meet both B and C on the bridge," I said. "Besides, the B group is really going to get ticked off if the C group sights a bear and they don't."

"The C group didn't complain when the A group dragged everyone to their stupid rain forest with the B group," he growled.

"The A group really gets on your nerves," I said.

"You're the A group," he said.

I was losing it.

All of this sounds grim, but somehow I have a strange feeling that in terms of an expedition, this cruise was a roaring success. People on these trips expect to suffer. It's part of the adventure. Part of the seduction. Could you come back from planting a flag on the summit of Mount Everest without frostbite? Could you find the mouth of the Nile without getting malaria? Could you return home from a fishing expedition to Alaska with salmon that didn't cost $516.12 a pound?

On the last day, as we were on our way to Prince Rupert, both of us were once again in our beds nauseated beyond belief from the rolling seas. In a few hours all of this would be a bad memory. I rolled over and said to my husband, "Do you know what I am going to do before we make port?"

"What?" he asked.

"I'm going to do something on behalf of all these poor unfortunates who survived on this bucket for two weeks. I am going to leave this cabin, march straight to the captain's deck, take his palm tree out of the pot, and throw it overboard. Then I am going to knock on his door and announce, 'Captain! I have just thrown your—'"

"You're not going to do that," he said tiredly.

He was right. I didn't do that.

But there hasn't been a day since that I don't hate myself for not doing it.

Working Vacations

Combining work and play on a vacation never worked for me. Doctors are good at it. They go on a cruise, swim all morning, and laze around the pool. Around two, they attend a lecture on how to treat "Statement Printout Anxiety" and later view a style show on paper gowns. They dance until two a.m. and write the whole thing off.

On a couple of occasions, I have been lured into doing a book tour in some country where I am promised some free time on my own. In your dreams. You try to sell books to 3 million sheep in New Zealand and tell me how much time you have to relax.

A few books ago, I toured Australia and New Zealand for a month. Beginning at Perth, I worked my way across Australia's 2,966,200 square miles.

Do you think I saw Mel Gibson? Colleen McCullough? Or Crocodile Dundee throwing a few shrimp on the barbie? Get real.

I saw one koala bear with runny eyes, bubbling sulfa at Rotorua, a staged Maori dance at the hotel, a geothermal plant, and two kangaroos from the car. Oh yes, I bumped into Jim Nabors and Jackie Collins on a talk show.

It was the same in London. I heard people talk of a place where you could see the crown jewels of Britain. I heard there was a beautiful river Thames that ran through the city and that the queen lived in a palace with guards at the gate.

I didn't so much as get to the hat factory where they made all those hats that Princess Di and Fergie wear to deliver their babies in. Where was I? I was inside a building called the BBC. Every morning I would sit in a little room by myself with a pair of headphones. When a little red light went on, I would say, "Good morning, Ireland" or "Good morning, Wales" and I would talk about my book. For that, I shaved my legs.

It is rare when your work takes you to a place you really want to go. It is doubly rare when your reason for being there opens doors to you that you would never get through if you were on holiday.

Such was the case with Russia.

Russia

When my husband and I made our first trip to Russia in 1977, the journey had all the giddiness of being extradited to a Georgia penal institution. We were guarded closely, counted every time we went to the bathroom, and sequestered by Intourist services. God forbid we would see or talk with a Soviet citizen.

From the time our tour group left the ship in Leningrad, where we boarded the Red Arrow train to Moscow, we were never left alone. If Russians were interested in us, they didn't show it. Their eyes focused on the ground in front of them. We were mothered through Red Square, folkloric performances, and state shopping stores. We were fed in private dining rooms. It was reminiscent of being in a kindergarten class and holding hands in a single file when you visited the airport.

Since our time in Moscow was short, three couples were assigned to a dayroom at an Intourist hotel to "freshen up." As my husband and I sat on a bed in the awkward silence of being with four other people we didn't know, the young woman from Canada broke the silence with, "Anyone for a nooner?" I could visualize a poor KGB agent in a basement somewhere rummaging through English dictionaries trying to figure out what a "nooner" was.

Visiting this beige, bland, unleavened strip of Europe was akin to chewing on a stalk of celery—no enjoyment, but you could at least say you ate. I left it with a burning curiosity about the people who lived in those stark, colorless high-rises. Who were these emotionless faces we saw from the windows of touring buses that never slowed down? Maybe if I had been able to look into just one pair of eyes, I could have gotten a handle on what they were all about.

It was to be ten years before we returned to Russia. We were on a cruise and made port in a small town called Nakhodka, the eastern terminus of the Trans-Siberian Railway. Word of glasnost and perestroika had reached the cruise ships. The rumor had filtered down to Nakhodka . . . but just barely.

I had an aunt whom we once called to tell her we were going to drop by for a visit for a few hours. With fifteen hours' notice, my aunt wallpapered the entire house, painted the lawn furniture, landscaped the front and back yards, fixed the toilet, hung new draperies, plastered the kitchen, laid new carpet throughout, had her hair cut, and bought a new grill to cook out. Nakhodka people did the same thing.

An invasion of tourists from an American cruise ship was not a thing that happened every day in this little town and they were going to make it memorable. They put together a luncheon where the tables groaned with food. A small orchestra played at eighty-six decibels. Hostesses smiled and offered you drinks. They thought of everything but chairs and silverware.

For entertainment, they staged a gymnastic exhibition in the school gym. As we filed in, we nearly passed out from the paint fumes, but we slid onto the bright blue benches to watch Russian children perform with the style and grace for which they are noted. When they finished, my husband leaned over and said, "We can go now." I whispered back, "You can go. My shoes are stuck to the floor." Looking around, I realized they weren't the only things embedded in the paint. Those who couldn't get a seat carried away paint on their slacks and sweaters from brushing against the doorways.

All of it was awkward—like two countries on a blind date. But then an extraordinary thing happened as it can only when people are left to their own devices. Our buses had pulled up to the Nakhodka Museum, a dreary collection of maritime memorabilia and restrooms that didn't work. As the Americans sat on the steps, a few took yet another picture of yet another Lenin statue that dominated the square. Mostly, we were killing time. From a distance came a parade of the town's citizens. Mothers in their best dresses pushed babies in strollers. Men appeared in suits and ties, and from somewhere a group of musicians started to play music on the museum steps. The townspeople made a circle and began to dance for us. The Americans made the circle even larger. We couldn't begin to communicate with one another, but somehow there was a strong feeling that if we both reached out, we would remember this day for a long time.

I did.

The following year I was invited to Russia along with eight other American women to have a dialogue with members of the Soviet Women's Committee. It was a working visit sparked by Ellen Levine, editor of *Woman's Day* magazine, and an organization called Peace Links created by Betty Bumpers of Arkansas. We hoped the meeting would result in an exchange of problems, followed by an exchange of solutions.

As I sat at the long table, tilted on the side of the Russians by sheer numbers, I at last had a chance to look into the eyes of these people. Maybe if we cried about the same things and laughed about the same things there was hope for the world.

Since I was introduced as a humorist, I began my remarks by telling them that the major problem of American women was that for every pair of socks put into the washer, only one sock came back. We figured it went to live with Jesus.

It wasn't the first time I had told a joke and died. It was, however, the first time I felt they were going to outline my body in chalk. How could Russian women possibly relate to washing machine stories when no one owned one?

Moving right along, I told them the second major problem in America was men who sat around and watched one hundred and eighty-seven football games a weekend. At this point, the entire Russian delegation snapped to life and the chairman interrupted, "Mrs. Bombeck, you have just touched upon a global problem. What do you do in America about husbands who watch too much TV?"

I told her I had mine declared legally dead and his estate probated.

The laughter came. It was a Laughnost breakthrough. From there on in, we became a good-ole-girls network trying to pinpoint our concerns and how we could deal effectively with them.

One woman told us how Russian women were given the incentive of 200 rubles ($336 in U.S. currency) for giving birth to triplets. She added dryly, "You don't see anyone racing for the door, do you?"

Another one complained about the reticence of the Russians to talk about sex. "There is no sex education taught in schools. My only instruction was from my mother who said, 'You'll get sick of the whole business soon enough.'" (The unmarried American delegate on my left mumbled, "Don't I wish." The translator broke up.)

At one point, one of the women, who held a doctorate in education, excused herself from the table. When we asked where she was going, we were told her grandchild was home ill and she wanted to check on him. They had caring grandmothers . . . even in the Evil Empire. Imagine that.

As I sat there day after day wearing headphones, listening to the interpreter struggle to make our words relevant, I wondered if we could establish a meaningful rapport with a nation that had never seen raisins dance in dark glasses on TV . . . never had a garage sale . . . never played bingo in the church basement.

I remembered the long lines of people I had seen on Gorky Street on my way to the offices of the committee. I recall thinking if I was standing in the early morning frost for hours, there had better be a pair of *Phantom of the Opera* tickets at the end of it or a ride on Magic Mountain.

Was it possible that out of our uncommon lives we shared common problems? We didn't have a choice. If we really loved our children, then we had to start reaching out to one another.

When you've been adversaries for so long, it's hard to show your warts. Each country had them. It was only a matter of who was going to show theirs first. It was a slow process. We admitted American women were not in our Constitution. Russian women were in their Constitution. They admitted the day care centers that were supposed to be years ahead of ours had a lot of problems. We admitted to a high divorce rate. They allowed there was a serious drinking problem among Soviet men. They had guilt. We had guilt. We would like to get rid of toys that depicted Russians as villains. They expressed shock because they had never had warlike toys to begin with.

Slowly, almost shyly, they began to ask about our system, especially about how we provided so much counseling to our people. We talked to them about "volunteerism." The word didn't even translate. The closest we came was "compassion." We told them helping one another was what Americans did best.

They pointed out they heard we put our elderly parents into homes and ignored them.

They didn't do that. We pointed out they didn't mainstream their disabled. They burst with pride that changes were abounding in the Soviet Union. I asked them how many Jews were represented on their Women's Soviet Committee and there was a long silence. "The weaker our men get, the stronger we become," they said. We pointed out their country, like ours, is run primarily by men.

The glaring difference between the present Moscow and the one of a few years ago was the freedom with which we moved through the city. We availed ourselves of the circus, the Bolshoi Ballet, and the daily search for food.

You can only have so many hot dogs for breakfast and then you go into junk food shock. We had to have real food. Through conscientious whining, we found out that a cooperative restaurant (one that is privately owned) in Moscow served Sara Lee cheesecake. On a scale of one to ten in euphoria, it was just under an arms agreement. We all piled into taxicabs and made our way to the restaurant.

OK, so the bread was bad, the salad was bad, the fish was bad, but we knew there was a big finish. They were out of cheesecake.

Many times before travelers go to a country, they pack too much baggage—not necessarily clothes, but impressions of what the people are going to be like and how they will fit the stereotype fashioned for them. In my mind, I visualized

Russian women with skinny legs, big boobs, and no waistline draped in the same print dress. In fact, there was a commercial shown in America depicting industrial-strength Soviet women that only reinforced my perception. It was a fashion show in which every Russian woman had the same floral shift, and the only way you knew the outfit was different was that she carried a beach-ball for "svimvear" or a flashlight for "evening vear."

I was wrong. Russian women may not be as trendy as American women, but they care about what they look like as much as other women throughout the world. They are limited only by budget and availability of merchandise. They have waistlines and trim ankles, and they wear makeup effectively. It was a surprise for me to hear they are "into" spas and have been for years.

Personally, I am a spa freak. Show me a place where you touch your ear to your knee one hundred forty-five times an hour, balance your body in the air on your shoulders and squeeze your buttocks, sit naked in a Jacuzzi, eat oat breath mints and drink herbal tea, and I will pay $1,500 a week to go there.

I arrive with suitcases filled with cute little coordinated outfits that I change six times a day. I don't read a newspaper or watch TV. My focus is my body and whether or not I'm a summer, fall, autumn, or spring "color." I go early to the gym and get my spot all staked out. (An evil woman once snapped at me, "If I had known it was so territorial, I'd have wet on my mat!") I spend all my evenings writing down recipes which I will never use, popping water pills, and committing my cholesterol number to memory.

Spas in America are usually limited to women who don't need them, but who want to be pampered and told they don't need them. They just like the elegance of sitting around listening to Japanese music piped into their pillows, rose petals on their tofu, and fifty-pound terry cloth robes.

With this picture in mind, I stood before a red brick Russian bath that could have been the oldest school building in New York City. It made a condemned Y look like La Costa. There were four of us who at this point concurred that coming here was one of the bravest things we had ever done. We didn't know a single word of Russian between us, had no idea how we were going to bluff our way through this day once we left the cab. At best, we could spend a luxurious afternoon. At worst, we could set Russian relations back two hundred years.

We checked our coats and waited. Several minutes had passed when a woman summoned us to follow her to a large room with little cubicles. She then went through a pantomime of taking off her clothes over her head. No one spoke as we looked at one another. She did it again and disappeared. Finally, one of our delegates said, "I think she wants us to take our clothes off."

"Mary-Lou," I said, "if you are wrong, this is going to be the longest day of our lives."

Once we were in the buff, we were led to a large room and abandoned. Milling around us were thirty or more buck-naked Soviet women wearing wool ski caps. It was enough to take the sight out of a good eye. They looked us over and instinctively knew we were Americans and decided to take us under their wings.

We didn't have ski caps to protect our heads from the heat of the sauna, so they wrapped towels around our skulls. We would have followed them anywhere. When they scrubbed their feet, we scrubbed our feet. When they grabbed eucalyptus branches to flog themselves in the steam bath, so did we. When they sat in the sauna and dehydrated, we clung to them the way a nylon slip sticks to pantyhose. When they fell into the cold, green pool, we followed. Later, we all agreed that summit meetings between world leaders should be conducted in the nude—to keep everything in perspective. It's a great equalizer.

Their facials are in Baskin-Robbins flavors. I chose the strawberry because one of the attendants showed me a picture of Linda Evans and then pointed to the strawberry mix. Gorbachev should have her optimism.

When a magazine editor asked in amazement why we went to a Russian bath and what I discovered about Soviet women there, I said, "It reaffirmed what I have always known . . . all women are not created equal."

Or were we? Once you have looked into the eyes of people in a foreign country, you realize you all want the same thing: food on your table, love in your marriage, healthy children, laughter, freedom to be. The religion, the ideology, and the government may be different, but the dreams are all the same.

We were nearing our last hours in Moscow. I went to my hotel room to pack. It was an enormous room, a two-room suite, actually, that was so . . . Russian. The ceilings were high and ornate; there was bric-a-brac everywhere. Antique lamps were topped by shades with fringe. Hardwood floors gleamed. A large piano dominated the room. (It had no insides.) I picked up the last of the bottled water I had brought from New York (I couldn't find any in Russia) and went to the window before slugging it down. The room overlooked the Kremlin.

I folded the used towels in the bathroom, emptied the ashtrays bulging with candy wrappers (I had brought candy to give to the children, but I needed it worse than they did), and closed the giant doors of the ornate armoire. Pausing at the door before leaving, I walked back into the room and poised myself over one of the lamps before speaking into it. "Forget the extra towels I ordered. I'm leaving today. I had a nice time."

I don't know if the room was bugged or not, but if we love children, someone has to give.

A
Jack Nicholson
Wheat Toast
Day

In a film called *Five Easy Pieces*, Jack Nicholson has a classic scene in a diner. When he orders two pieces of wheat toast, he is told it isn't on the menu and they cannot possibly make an exception.

He says to the waitress, "Let me make it easy for you. I'll have the chicken salad sandwich on wheat bread. Hold the mayonnaise, hold the lettuce and the chicken salad, and toast the bread."

Eating on a vacation is often a challenge. Shortages, customs, unrecognizable spices, ethnic favorites, lack of health standards. All are a part of the foraging process. Sometimes it's a real cerebral experience.

While in Jerusalem, I called room service on a

Friday night to order something light for dinner.

"I'll have a grilled cheese sandwich and a bowl of matzo ball soup," I said.

The voice of room service said, "I cannot do that. This is Shabbat." (Shabbat is the Jewish sabbath observance from sundown on Friday to sundown on Saturday.)

"What does that mean?" I asked.

"That means we observe kosher dietary laws. We cannot serve a dairy product with the soup and the soup would have to be served separately. They cannot be delivered on the same tray, nor can they be in the room at the same time. Also, we do not do manual labor on Shabbat and cannot operate the toaster."

"I see," I said. "Then could you bring a bowl of soup to my room? Then deliver me a plain cheese sandwich on whole wheat bread and leave it in the hallway. When I am finished with the soup, I will put the bowl in the hallway and bring in the sandwich." It was perfectly acceptable and no laws were broken.

There is always a way.

Montserrat

The kids were oohing and aahing over the swimming pool tucked underneath the villa. My husband was in a state of excitement at being able to bring in Dan Rather on the large TV set in the living room. Other family members and friends were exploring the fantastic view from the large porch that overlooked the Caribbean.

I was in the kitchen slumped in a chair wondering how I was going to feed ten people with one box of powdered milk, one jar of jelly, three frozen chicken fillets, one small jar of instant coffee, and a bottle of Scotch.

When we leased the villa, we were assured the staff would stock provisions for the first day until we got our bearings. The agreement also listed a caretaker in residence and maid service four days a week.

The caretaker was a young islander who called himself Soul Man. He was born in Montserrat and had the deal of his life. He had his own digs, used the big house when no one was there, and had use of a car. All he had to do for all of this was to smile and cut the grass every two weeks.

"I have to make a trip into town for groceries," I told Soul Man. "I cannot possibly feed ten people with this. Do you suppose you could give me a hand?"

The smile never left his handsome face. "Ooooooh, bad time to go to the store. It's the day after Christmas."

"I know that, but tomorrow is Sunday and we're going to be in big trouble by then."

Soul Man drove me to a large warehouse of sorts where cases of beer and soft drinks were stacked to the ceiling. At one end were a few sparsely stocked shelves. All the milk was powdered. There were no fresh vegetables or fruits and only a few loaves of bread.

"How about meats?" I asked.

He smiled and pointed to a chest freezer. I opened it and stared in. It was barren with the exception of five inches of frost and three naked chickens that had been dressed and tossed in . . . no bags, no wrappings, no nothing. Their positions were unnatural. I pulled them out and headed to the checkout with them in my cart.

The moment the cashier saw the chickens she began to scream at me. "What is she saying?" I asked Soul Man.

"She says those are her chickens. She has been saving them until she gets off work. They are not for sale."

For the first day or so, we ate like we were a lost platoon on maneuvers. I apologized and said come Monday I would go to a real store.

On Monday, when I approached Soul Man, he said, "Ooooooh, bad time to go to store on Monday. It's the day of the beauty pageant in Montserrat. Everything closed."

"Maybe when Carla the maid comes in she will know of a store that is open," I said.

"Carla will not come in today. I told you, it's the day of the beauty pageant."

"Is she in it?" I asked.

He thought I was joking and smiled.

During the next day or so we visited several grocery stores, each one more depressing than the one before. We scoured the phone book and saw a full-page ad for a meat market. When we got there, it was the size of an airline restroom and had nothing. We ate a lot of bread and applesauce and cookies.

But it was the instant coffee that drove us crazy. All of us are "real coffee" drinkers. We searched the house from top to bottom looking for some kind of a pot to brew coffee in. No success. On our next trip to town, we vowed to get a coffeepot for "real coffee."

On the fourth day, one of our guests unearthed a seven-pound ham. I figured that would give us a dinner, plus sandwiches for a day or so. By the time the fat cooked down, we were lucky to have enough to flavor green beans. If we had been able to get green beans.

Carla didn't come on the next working day because it was Jump-Up Festival in Montserrat. I had no idea what that was, but if they served snow cones on the street or even a hot dog, it was worth cleaning my own house and doing my own laundry. We went to Jump-Up Festival but never found a street vendor.

When we asked strangers where they shopped, they were rather vague and guarded about where they got their food. One woman advised I should go to the open market if I wanted fresh fruits and vegetables. "But go early," she warned.

I barely slept just thinking about an outdoor market. I don't even like salads. Catsup every week or so is the only vegetable I eat with any regularity. But the idea of not seeing a tomato or a piece of lettuce for a week just seemed unnatural.

In the small, dark hours of the morning, my

husband and I headed to market with our large baskets in tow. We joined the small group of people milling around. At one counter, a salesperson stood guard over thirty-seven little string beans. I counted them.

"I'll take all the string beans you have," I said, opening my purse.

She looked at me closely like she was interviewing a surrogate mother. "If I sell you the string beans, you have to take the tomato."

The tomato was bruised beyond description. "I don't want the tomato," I said.

"Then you don't get the string beans." She sniffed and went on to the next customer. I ran behind her pleading my case. I couldn't believe it. I was groveling for thirty-seven lousy beans for ten people!

I never worked so hard for food in my life. I got four potatoes at one stand, three tomatoes at another, two heads of romaine lettuce, and a bunch of green bananas that are still on the kitchen countertop in Montserrat ripening to this day.

"Where do you buy meat?" I kept asking. Finally, one man motioned to the alley behind the market. I walked up and down until I found a door with a freezer inside.

"Hamburger?" I asked.

The man smiled and gave me a box full of frozen patties. I had the feeling they were any kind of meat you wanted them to be.

A couple of our guests were in charge of tracking down a coffeepot, which was like telling Columbus, "Go find a new world." An owner of one of the stores finally said, "Look, I've got an electric coffeepot I never use. I'll sell it to you for $40."

There was a reason why he never used it. The current in Montserrat was all wrong for it and it took hours for the water to filter through the coffee. One of us would have to set the alarm for two A.M. to start the coffee so it would be there for breakfast.

After a while, it was amazing how the Swiss Family Wilderness actually survived. We got pretty creative. At lunch one day we had potato salad, canned tuna salad, and canned shrimp salad. If anyone was allergic to mayonnaise, he'd have starved to death. Another time we planned a picnic around beef jerky and oatmeal cookies. It was never "What did you do today?" It was, "What did you find to eat today?"

Through conscientious dedication, we found a Sara Lee outlet, an ice cream connection, and a bakery. The big news is we found a turkey for New Year's. All of us wrote cards home sharing that find.

One morning of the second week, a woman appeared at the villa and started to dust the dining room. It was the elusive Carla, a Montserrat native species we thought was extinct. She explained she missed two days ago because of New Year's. We said we understood. We asked her if there was one great grocery store we hadn't found yet and she said, "No." Then she added, "I won't be in on Friday. It's my birthday."

We tried to rationalize the shortage of food on Montserrat. There was food on Antigua, Guadeloupe, and other islands around it. Maybe eating was something that never got important to them. I remember picking up a large circle of white enclosed in cellophane and asking the grocery clerk what it was. She said, "It's icing for the cake. After you have baked a cake, you just drop it on." I never figured them for the Stepford Wives . . . especially Carla. Maybe we were trying to re-create the home we had just left. Most travelers are like that when it comes to their stomachs.

It's interesting what you think about when you mention the name of a place you've visited. I barely remember the beaches, the weather, or the history of Montserrat. I think about ten people who for one shining moment thought they had come to Camelot and ended up with beef jerky and oatmeal cookies.

The night before we left the island retreat, my husband said, "Don't forget to clean out the refrigerator." What a kidder. It had been cleaned out since the day we arrived.

"How early do we leave in the morning?" I asked.

"The plane takes off at seven-thirty A.M.," he answered.

I jumped up. "Why didn't you tell me earlier? The coffee will never get done."

Great Barrier Reef

We have never been your basic beach family. We don't know what to do with ourselves.

There is a picture of us taken in Hawaii several years ago on our visit to the island of Kauai. While other fun-seekers around us were stretched out comatose on towels, their basted bodies toasted brown by the sun, our family was a study in motion. The dog was hyper from chasing a Frisbee. Our sons were playing volleyball. Our daughter was building the Trump Tower in the sand. My husband was swathed in towels balancing our checkbook. I was hooking a rug.

We have slides of us doing crossword puzzles on the beach in Tahiti, buying dresses from vendors in Cabo San Lucas, and using metal detectors in search of loose change in Fiji. Other than the fact that we are all keeping busy, there is another common thread running through the pictures. I am wearing the same bathing suit.

It is a no-nonsense, one-piece, blue and white polka dot with industrial strength straps, a generous drape over the stomach, and enough rubber in the bra to support an eighteen-wheeler.

If I weren't such a phony, I'd probably admit that's the real reason I don't "do beaches." They're infested with women from the current *Sports Illustrated* swimwear edition. I have cooked bigger turkeys than most of them.

The idea of actually going into the water came about on a Caribbean cruise when one of the ports was St. Thomas. My husband wanted me to take a short course in scuba diving, but when I heard you had to do a little math I told him if I wanted to use my brain on vacation, I'd stay in my cabin and watch "Jeopardy." Instead, I took a bus to a beach where a young kid spit into a mask, placed it over my face, and told me to float and I would probably see Lloyd Bridges. I fell in love with snorkeling. I wasn't good at it, but I loved it. It was a world I had never seen before.

When we made plans to take the family to the Great Barrier Reef off the coast of Australia, I even went so far as to try to replace my fifteen-year-old swimsuit.

I brushed by the racks of bikinis that looked like snack crackers and wondered who designed these things. Swimsuit manufacturers were out to lunch. Did they honestly believe that all women are endowed with the same equipment? Couldn't they figure out that when a stomach is covered with gold lamé it looks like the Capitol dome? Or that many women have erosion on their bodies that looks like a relief map of California's freeways?

My hand brushed by a little one-piece black suit that looked promising. In the fitting room, it slipped over my body. The neck was high enough, but the legs of the suit went all the way up to my armpits. I figured no one at the Great Barrier Reef had seen my blue and white polka dot number.

Our destination was Heron Island, one of two island resorts that is actually on the reef. It formerly housed a turtle soup factory, but that didn't work out, and in 1932, someone figured out it had tourist potential.

At Gladstone, Australia, a woman quickly rushed us onto the tarmac into a waiting helicopter for the trip. As an afterthought, she tossed in a couple of packets and said, "By the way, these are your parachute packs. Please don't inflate them until after you leave the plane." I had no intention of leaving the plane.

An hour later, we were at one of the most beautiful islands I had ever set eyes on. It was our kind of beach. No one, but no one, was sitting idly in the sun. Everyone was busy. Children and adults wearing tennis shoes were scouring the shallow reefs with glass-bottom buckets looking for sea life. Snorkelers dotted the water, and large rubber boats carried scores of divers to blue waters rich with sea life.

I quickly changed into my suit, spit on my mask, put it over my face, and floated out to sea. Within minutes, my older son tapped me on the shoulder and as I lifted my face out of the water, I saw him waving two feet of fat snake in front of my eyes. "It's a sea slug," he yelled. I wanted to hurt him. My husband said, "Don't scare your mother like that." I was a little more direct. "You-are-out-of-the-will!" I shouted.

On an excursion in the glass-bottom boat I saw things that I had never seen in the gentle coves of St. Thomas. These fish had large mouths and jagged teeth. There were slimy eels and humongous shadows cast by manta rays. This was not good.

With each day my enthusiasm for exploring the deep became less and less. It was a case of knowing too much. Then one afternoon, we were poking around the beach when my husband said, "I think I'll snorkel a bit before lunch." He was out there about an hour or so when I said to the kids, "Look, your father is only in four feet of water muddling around. He'll be all right. Let's have lunch."

Halfway through the meal, their father joined us, visibly shaken. He had been snorkeling when a large shark began to encircle him. The waiter standing nearby smiled and said, "This isn't Sea World, you know. It's the South Pacific."

He was absolutely right. What did we know about what lurked down there? We didn't know which coral to touch or which fish to pet. All we knew was Jacques Cousteau sitting around a table eating lobster and talking French.

The next day, we were at the beach early.

The kids were playing cards. My husband was tallying up our credit card expenses. I was needle-pointing a pillow top of John Wayne.

Time to Go Home

No one has to tell you on a vacation when it is time to go home.

It's nothing obvious like ripping out your last traveler's check or running out of malaria pills.

It can be as simple as standing in a line waiting for a bullet train in Japan, and suddenly you are being shoved aside and you yell, "Those pushy French again! This isn't the Maginot Line you're defending, sweetie, it's only a seat on a commuter train!"

You're testy and you know it.

You are sick of being served sheep's eyeballs and having some idiot say, "Bloomingdale's sells this as a delicacy in their Christmas catalog." If someone tells you an icon is over 2 million years old and is only steps from the bus, you yawn and say, "Describe it to me." Your homing instincts kick in. A carnival could fill the streets outside your hotel window and you opt to stay in your room and watch CNN.

You're bored with your wardrobe and your hair. You're exhausted from packing and rearranging all those stupid souvenirs you couldn't live without, and you're fed up to here with people quoting battles and dates.

My husband can always tell when I'm on Vacation Overload. I turn into Leona Helmsley.

You know the ads that used to appear in the airline magazines, where the headline reads SPOTLESS! BUT NOT TO LEONA HELMSLEY. CAN YOU SEE WHY?

I know why! There are four hand towels and two bath towels hung on the bar in my bathroom and there should be four bath towels to go with the four hand towels. Incompetent sows.

I don't know why I take everything out on my surroundings, but I do. If my soap is the size of a credit card, I cry. If my bedspread weighs a hundred and thirty-seven pounds and I have to remove it, I have a temper tantrum, and if the paper strip across the toilet seat is broken, I fall apart.

My hotel room is either too big or too small. There is no pleasing me on the last days of a vacation. It's someone's law—the shorter your stay, the more elaborate your room.

In Tokyo, we checked into a suite that had a boardroom table the size of my entire house, a bar, a concert grand piano, and five bathrooms. The ceiling over one of the tubs was mirrored.

"It figures," I groused. "We're staying here one night. Why couldn't we have had these accommodations in Adelaide, Australia when we were jammed in a broom closet for a week and had to turn off the TV set with our toes? Hurry up and unpack so I can sit in a tub, look at the ceiling, and watch my cellulite float."

In Istanbul, I remember pausing just outside the room we had been assigned. I noted a small gold plate on the door that read Julio Iglesias Room. I kicked open the door. There were twin beds six inches off the floor, draped in tired royal blue satin ruffled spreads. The blue satin curtains sagged like a dirty diaper and had a few pins missing. The carpet was threadbare, the refrigerator door was ajar, and the radiator was a monument to ugly. "I don't care if Julio Iglesias comes with the bed," I snapped, "I'm leaving."

Usually, I am not like this. Accommodations are a part of the adventure. We have stayed in the best and the worst of them. We have been guests in Paradise where there is a hair dryer on the wall, a terrycloth robe on a hook, heated towel racks, toilet paper that is folded over into points, and a picture over the sofa of an eyeball in shades of green with a brass plate that reads *Phoebe In Love*.

We have also visited Flop City with a bottle opener on the door, a room key that dangles from a piece of wood the size of a tree trunk, a nude woman fashioned into a lamp with the switch in her navel, and nothing on the wall but the room rates.

During the last days of a vacation I form pictures of my house in my mind. For no apparent reason I will be looking at a prehistoric pot somewhere and I will say to my husband, "Did you turn off the coffeepot when we left?"

This makes him as anxious to get home as I am.

You can always tell when vacationers are going or coming. Travelers who are at the beginning of a trip laugh and tell jokes. Their clothes match. They see a line and they go to the end of it.

Those returning are impatient. Every plane they board is like the last one out of Baghdad and they are going to be on it.

Something else happens to me that I cannot explain. I become as American as the Fourth of July. I can't wait to see the Energizer rabbit march across the TV screen or Mayor Dinkins's picture welcoming me to New York City. I want to hear cabdrivers yell, "Get out of my face!" I want to eat hamburgers so fat I can barely fit them in my mouth. I want to hear English and see signs I can read and spend "real" money. I want Dan Rather to tell me how the world has fared in my absence. I want to smell clean clothes, drink tap water, and sleep in my own bed.

But reentering the world you have left for two or three weeks is not an easy thing. One must pay a price for exploring new cultures. You cannot just get on a plane, arrive home, and pick up life where you left it. You first have to go through a rite of passage, a ritual as old as man himself. It is called jet lag.

Jet Lag

Jet lag is a temporary disruption of the body's normal biological rhythms after high-speed air travel through several time zones.

That's a classy way of saying your body will never be the same again. You will sleep when everyone else is awake, camp outside supermarkets at three A.M. waiting for them to open, nod off during a root canal, and possibly damage your biological clock and give birth at the age of fifty-three. You could die from jet lag.

There have been a couple of feeble attempts to deal with the malady. A drug called Melatonin has been used effectively on sheep, but how many sheep do you know who are frequent flyers?

A few years ago when scientists began to take

the problem seriously, they even did some research and discovered that eating and drinking light and exercising helped make the transition from time zone to time zone easier. Like I'm going to sit in my seat and pretend I'm rowing a boat or raise my knees to my chin or roll my shoulders back and forth. Get outta here! The only aerobic exercise anyone gets on a plane is disengaging oneself from the jaws of the folding door of the restroom which threatens to digest you.

My husband has an interesting theory. He figures if he refuses to change his watch he can play around with the difference and eventually catch up an hour at a time.

The real truth is a couple of years ago the kids bought him a runner's watch for Father's Day. He never could set it. It's easier to pop out to Stonehenge and measure shadows than it is to get the right time out of him. Ask him the hour and prepare to grow old.

We were on the way back from Tokyo and I made the mistake of asking him the time. He said, "Wait a minute. I have to find my glasses." After several minutes of searching, he said, "Do you have a pencil handy?" Then he proceeded to calculate, tabulate, subtract, and divide, and by the time he came up with the time, we were in another time zone. Finally he said, "Why do you want to know?"

I said, "I want to know when to sleep."

He said, "Your body will tell you."

I must have sat there an hour before my body said, "It's nine P.M., Erma, and in another hour I am going to crash."

I said to my body, "You know, you'd be doing me a big favor if you could just stay awake and eat a six-course dinner and watch *Jewel of the Nile*. Trust me, you'll be a better person for it."

My body said, "Why should I believe you? That's what you told me the year you took me to Australia. I've never been the same."

"Give me a break," I pleaded. "Do I ask you for much?"

Halfway through *Jewel of the Nile,* my body defied me and dozed off. Four hours later the lights of the plane went on and the steward announced, "Breakfast."

My body jerked to attention and said, "What are you trying to pull, dimbulb? I just ate. Besides, you know I sleep on Sundays."

"It's not Sunday, it's Monday. Now have a hard roll and shut up!"

My body didn't speak to me for a long time. As we approached Hawaii, I nudged it again and whispered, "Time to eat breakfast."

I heard it mumble, "We did that, remember?"

"Well, do it again." We were at odds with one another the entire trip home. I made my legs walk when they were asleep, closed my eyes when they were wide open, ate dinner in the A.M. and breakfast in the P.M., trying to adjust.

In Los Angeles, as the plane emptied, it occurred to me we looked like a transport of derelicts. There was a steady stream of passengers with eyes that sparkled under a rosy glaze, disheveled clothes, twisted hair that stood on end, and enough bags under their eyes to keep twenty porters employed for a year. They had the look of people with no will to live.

Homecoming

Vacations fade fast. Their memories are obliterated by little things. You arrive home to discover your car has died. Neighbors inform you the power went off while you were gone and your freezer will smell like a fertilizer plant when you open the door. Somehow, it escaped someone's attention that your garden hose was left running and floated your house to a new zip code.

If all that doesn't take the hats and horns out of your trip, distribution of the souvenirs will.

Rarely does anyone appreciate what you have gone through to get these gifts home. They have no meaning. The primitive necklace that you bargained for in Tanzania is held at arm's length by a friend who sniffs, "Is this another one of these things that I have to put in the freezer first to kill bugs?"

Children are the worst. I once babied a large Mexican hat the size of a satellite dish. It wouldn't fit under the seat on the plane or in the overhead bin. I had to wear it most of the time. Our son looked at it, said it smelled, and kicked it under his bed.

The fur drum we dragged home for one of them from the Bahamas literally came alive when we turned the furnace on. We saw it scaling the wall one day.

A couple of years ago when we returned from the Orient, I spread all my souvenirs out on the dining room table and circled it slowly for hours trying to figure out who deserved any of it.

My husband came into the room and said, "Did you give the silk kimono to your mother yet?"

"You know," I said slowly, "I have to think about that. She likes to get dressed as soon as she rolls out of bed. It would just hang there in her closet. Besides, it's not her color so I'm keeping it for myself."

"You could give her the tea set."

"I could, but I'm not. I don't have a nice tea set, and besides, I heard her say once that tea upsets her stomach."

"So you're going with the woodblock print," he said.

"I was until I got to thinking you would have to have been at the factory to appreciate all the work that goes into them. Actually, I've got the perfect spot for it in the living room."

"How about the glass necklace?"

"You really think so? I don't think Mother has the chest for it. I'll keep that for myself. I'm leaning toward the T-shirt."

"I thought you bought those for your aunts."

"We never see them," I said, "so I kept three for myself and decided to give each of them a pair of chopsticks."

"Smart idea. They're nice ones. They were expensive."

"On the other hand, I might have a dinner party with a theme some night. Maybe I'll give them a Christmas ornament and brochure on the history of the silkworm."

"They'll be choked up."

"What kind of a crack is that! Maybe I'll keep all of the T-shirts and give Mother a fan."

"I thought you were giving the fan to Brenda who watered your plants and brought in our mail."

"She's down to boxes of matches from the hotel. Look, it's not how much something cost, it's the thought that counts."

"So you're still looking for something for your mother."

I took the fan out of the box and opened it. It would just fit into my purse and I could . . .

I saw my husband looking at me. "Is that the best you can do for a woman who gave you life, raised you, and stood by you during the good times and the bad times of your life?"

I threw in a panda bear entwined around a pencil. "Now are you happy?" I asked.

One tries desperately to cling to joyous, carefree days and all the cultural enrichment you experienced on a trip, but it isn't easy with the inevitable post-vacation visit from Stan and Doris.

OK, so you don't expect to reenter your city on donkeys under a canopy of palms. And you certainly don't expect your friends to line the streets waiting for you to say something meaningful from a hillside. But is it too much to ask of a small group to listen to you talk about your trip and politely say, "That sounds like such fun. I hope you took pictures"?

Stan and Doris also travel and plan their vacations down to the last detail. They believe that timing is everything. When they visit St. Peter's in Rome, the Pope says Mass. When they fly over Hawaii, a volcano is erupting . . . on their side of the plane. It never rains on Stan and Doris. They plan it that way.

Not us. When we are standing in front of a panda bear giving birth, we are out of film. The day we view Old Faithful, the eruption has all the force of a radiator that blew its cap. When we are in Russia, Lenin's tomb is "leaking again and closed for repairs."

One year we returned from Greece to find Stan and Doris on our doorstep. "Tell! Tell!" they gushed. "What did you see?"

Happily, we recounted our three weeks in Greece—from the Acropolis and Mount Lycabettus to Constitution Square and the Royal Gardens. We burst with excitement over our visits to stadiums, archaeological museums, ruins, temples, and digs. When we finished, Stan looked at us and said, "You didn't eat at Syros Herculonburgers?"

We shook our heads.

"Then you didn't see Greece," he said. He turned to Doris. "Can you imagine the Bombecks going all the way to Greece and not eating at Syros Herculonburgers?"

Doris dropped into a chair like she had just been bitten by a viper. "You're kidding! Next thing you'll tell me is they didn't visit the Athos Flea Market."

"Where's the Athos Flea Market?" I asked.

"Oh Stan," she moaned, "I cannot believe what I am hearing. Tell me they didn't pay more than a dollar fifty for genuine icons at that little shop around the corner from the hotel."

As the memories of our travels fade, ironically, so do the moments of missed airplanes, drafty rooms, lost baggage, and death marches to view antiquity.

Along about December, something happens that once again revitalizes me and conjures up fantasies of faraway places. I realize I have nothing to live for. The white sales are over, my five-month cold has stabilized in my chest, and I have just received the Semples' annual Christmas barf-bulletin. This year's tome is written by their dog, Max, and signed with a paw print.

I remember Max. He came with them one year. I never saw the dog's face. It was either buried in someone's crotch or drinking from the toilet.

Anyway, at Christmas, Max, the wonder dog, faxes resumes of everyone in the family and what they have been doing for the past year. "Howard had hemorrhoid surgery but will be 'rarin' to go' again this summer. Fay got to see 'The Love Connection' last summer when they were visiting in California and 'Yes! Chuck Woolery is a hunk!'

"Howard Jr. is married and cannot come with them on vacation this year. Edwin is doing nicely at a halfway house, and the good news is that Sissy, who is divorced, will be able to make the trek with them to California this year along with her two babies." At the bottom of the sheet, Max has written in a P.S. under his paw print: "Fay and Howard told me to ask you if you still remember the gerbils."

It's a shame we won't be home.

Papua
New Guinea

It was the silence that awakened me . . . that same ominous chill you get when you stand at a bathroom door and yell to your kids, "What's going on in there?" and a small voice says, "Nothing."

The Kundiawa Inn, to be referred to in the future as Motel Hell, had survived the night. I dragged to the bathroom to see if I had done as well. My eyes looked and felt like they were on fire. One minute the fever was taking the curl out of my hair—the next, I was wrapping up in every piece of clothing I owned to stave off chills. I had lost an uncommon amount of weight. For a woman who gained three pounds during the delivery of an eight-pound baby, this was weird.

Steadying myself on the sink, I watched a trickle of brown water dribble out of the spigot. I fell into bed.

My husband was snapping a suitcase shut. "You going to be ready to check out in ten or fifteen minutes?" he asked.

"Don't ever say 'check out' to a sick person," I mumbled.

In the lobby, the only reminder of last night's war were three policemen having coffee. As I leaned against the wall for support, my foot hit a small alligator carved out of wood with his back hollowed out. Through parched lips I inquired, "Is this for sale?"

My husband materialized at my elbow to witness the transaction. "Thank God. I thought you were dead. What are you going to use it for?"

"I don't know," I said. "Dips . . . candy . . . nuts."

"The plane will never get off the ground with all this stuff."

Getting a plane off the ground in New Guinea is right up there with falling from the Empire State Building with a bungee cord tied around your ankles. Back home, their airstrips are known as unplowed fields. They are mined with ruts and rocks. They are also short. The plane usually aims toward the edge of a cliff. If the aircraft isn't airborne by the time it runs out of runway, the missionaries have a good day.

Flying low over the lush green jungles on our way home, I try to piece together not only the idiotic nightmare of the night before, but an answer to why we do this every year. Why do we leave an all-electric kitchen, people who speak our language, soft beds, safe drinking water, and toilets where we can sit on the seat?

What were we doing poking into other people's lives and cultures? Swatting their flies, worshipping at their shrines in our stocking feet, and lugging home Indonesian art to hang over our Santa Fe sofa?

Travel had long ago ceased to be just adventure and curiosity. For me, it had turned this planet into a small town—with a "Mayberry RFD" cast of people who had more in common than we had ever hoped was possible. We all had children who giggled . . . a belief in something bigger than ourselves . . . and a need to love and be loved back. It was a start.

Later that night as we walked into the lobby of one of Sydney, Australia's, five-star hotels, we must have looked like the Clampetts arriving in Beverly Hills.

Our shoes carried the mud of a hundred paths through the bush. Our clothes reeked of the smoke of a hundred campfires. Our bodies carried the sweat and dust of scores of villages and caves. As we blinked from the brightness of the lights from the elegant chandelier, I tried feebly to stuff the wooden alligator farther into my tote bag. A bellhop scurried to help me with another one of my souvenirs—a three-foot pig made out of skins. "Is this yours, sir?" *My God! He was talking to me!*

Somehow, I couldn't absorb it all. My reentry was too fast. The marble floors, the computers on the desk, the boutiques, the gift shops, the women in heels, the men exuding musk. It all seemed so unreal!

I just stood there in the middle of it all in a state of numbness. From across the lobby, a young, beautiful woman approached me, smiling. She looked like an album cover in her white tennis dress and dazzling smile. She smelled wonderful. "Hi," she said, "I'm Olivia Newton-John."

I sucked in my stomach (thank God, some reflexes were still working) and tried to explain that we looked this way because we had just returned from a world of skies blackened by fruit bats in the early morning hours . . . a place where giant frangipani trees rained pungent petals on you as you passed by and where exotic birds of dazzling colors ate off your plate at breakfast. But all I could do was to extend my hand and say, "We've been on vacation." It seemed to explain everything.

The encounter with Olivia Newton-John seemed to jar me back to civilization somehow. It gave me a grasp on reality. My roots needed color. I'd have to make an appointment the minute we got home. We had children. Should we call the kids in New York or take a chance on having a coronary when we saw the house? Would there be milk and bread for breakfast in the refrigerator? The only thing that stood between us and home now were the airport carousel and customs experiences.

The baggage claim at a port of entry is a study in subhuman behavior. I am convinced there will never be a viable hope for world peace until we can get two hundred people to claim their luggage from a carousel in an orderly fashion. This flight would be no different from the others.

When the plane landed, two hundred passengers sprang into the aisles like someone had just yelled "Fire!" They dragged carry-ons/coats/souvenirs/ children down miles of corridors until they reached baggage claim. Gasping and panting, they scoured the area and arm wrestled one another for the twelve luggage carts.

The people planted in cement closest to the carousel were the last to have their luggage come down the chute. Don't ask me why that is. It just is.

I was trampled to death by a man who believed his luggage would be the first piece off. If he were an experienced traveler, he would know that the first piece of luggage belongs to no one. It's just a dummy suitcase to give everyone hope.

The second and final hurdle between us and home was the customs line. This is where you stand around, spitting on your jewelry to make it look worn and in general trying to look as creditable as Walter Cronkite. I still felt lousy as I kicked our luggage forward inches at a time.

"You OK?" asked my husband.

"I'll make it," I said weakly.

The customs officer was riffling through the dirty underwear of the couple ahead of us. He held up a giant boomerang and turned it over several times.

The owner felt he had to defend it. "It's a boomerang," he said. There were at least thirty pairs of eyes focused on this fool who had lugged halfway around the world a crooked piece of wood that couldn't have gotten him 35 cents at a garage sale.

"I'm going to put it in my den," he announced to all of them. The customs officer just shook his head and waved him on. Somehow, we all knew he would never have the same feeling for the purchase as he had when he bought it.

We were next and I leaned against the counter for support. "Open 'em up," commanded the agent, pointing to our suitcases.

He worked like a surgeon . . . professional and without emotion as his fingers moved quickly under the plastic bags and among the shoes stuffed with socks and bras. Finally, both of his hands met in the bottom of the suitcase and he carefully extracted three elongated gourds and held them up for the entire terminal to view. Then he barked, "What are you going to do with all these penis gourds?"

It was like one of those scenes when E. F. Hutton talked and everyone listened. So that's what they were! I thought they were primitive artifacts they wore to add interest to a dull belt. By this time, decent people behind me were beginning to form opinions about us. Taking a deep breath, I said, "I'm going to use them for planters."

He motioned with his hand for me to move on and turned his attention to the next couple.

The lines from customs counters funneled into one large mess at the door where you had to show your passport and your declaration card before you were cleared to leave the terminal.

By this time, my face was on fire, my eyes were swollen half shut, and my lips were cracked with fever. The attendant flipped my passport open and looked from the photo to my face for confirmation.

"Good likeness." He smiled.

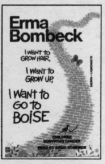